MW00835221

DATA PROCESSING IN

1980-1985

DATA PROCESSING IN
1980-1985

A Study of Potential
Limitations to Progress

T. A. Dolotta
Bell Laboratories

M. I. Bernstein
System Development Corporation

R. S. Dickson, Jr.
Phillips Petroleum Company

N. A. France
International Business Machines Corporation

B. A. Rosenblatt
Standard Oil Company of California

D. M. Smith
Exxon Corporation

T. B. Steel, Jr.
The Equitable Life Assurance Society of the United States

A WILEY-INTERSCIENCE PUBLICATION

JOHN WILEY & SONS, New York • London • Sydney • Toronto

This book was set in Times Roman on a Graphic Systems, Inc. phototypesetter. The phototypesetter was driven by a PDP 11/45 computer running under the UNIX operating system (a proprietary product of Bell Laboratories).

Published by John Wiley & Sons, Inc.

Copyright © 1976 by SHARE Inc.

All rights reserved. Published simultaneously in Canada.

No part of this book may be reproduced or transmitted in any form or by any means, electronic or mechanical, including photocopy, recording, or any information storage and retrieval system, without permission in writing from the copyright proprietor.

Library of Congress Cataloging in Publication Data:

Main entry under title:

Data processing in 1980-1985 : a study of
   potential limitations to progress.

   "A Wiley-Interscience publication."
   Bibliography: p.
   Includes index.
   1. Computer industry—United States.
   2. Business forecasting. I. Dolotta, T. A., 1934-

   HD9696.C63U5159   338.4'7'001640973   76-4783
   ISBN 0-471-21783-2
   ISBN 0-471-21786-7 pbk.

Printed in the United States of America

10 9 8 7 6 5 4 3 2 1

PREFACE

Once, when Sir Isaac Newton was asked how he made all of his discoveries, he replied: "If I have seen further than others, it is by standing upon the shoulders of Giants." Today, in the programming field, we mostly stand on each other's feet.
R. W. Hamming

Constant, rapid change is a fact of life in the data processing industry, and all those involved in it must maintain an awareness of where that industry is and where it is going. At times, professional survival may depend on a correct assessment of impending changes.

This book examines the problems that the data processing industry will be facing in the near future and outlines the kinds of actions that should be taken to meet these problems.

Specifically, we have tried to predict the environment and the status of the data processing industry in the years 1980 to 1985, with special emphasis on large, general-purpose, business-oriented data processing systems. We have tried to show how that status and the direction of the industry's development may *differ* from what most *users* of data processing facilities would like to see happen in that period, and we have tried to point out some of the reasons that may cause these differences to arise.

This book is the outcome of a study sponsored by SHARE Inc., an organization of users of large data processing systems, predominantly those supplied by the International Business Machines Corporation (IBM). Although we originally intended to present the results of our work to the SHARE Inc. membership as an internal report, it quickly became apparent that these results would be of real interest to the data processing community at large.

We have tried to illuminate the scope and interrelationships of the major issues and problems facing the entire data processing industry. We believe that this book, in addition to being of interest to the data processing community, will also be helpful to managers who are responsible for the allocation of resources to their respective data processing functions and will assist them in gaining a better understanding of these issues.

We claim that the data processing industry does indeed face major problems. Other groups have also perceived deficiencies in that industry's ability to respond to the increasingly strong demands being placed upon it. Concurrently with our efforts, the U.S. Armed Services Research Offices sponsored a symposium, in the fall of 1973, on the high cost of software. The keynote address at the 1974 National Computer Conference raised similar issues, and other groups are beginning to express concern about the productivity and the economics of various aspects of the data processing industry.

This book focuses on the *mainstream* of large, general-purpose, business-oriented data processing systems. We are concerned with the 1980's successors of computer series such as the IBM System/360 and System/370, UNIVAC 1100, Honeywell 6000, etc., rather than with the successors of small, stand-alone minicomputers, or successors of "supercomputers" such as the ILLIAC IV and the STAR-100. A common characteristic of the systems and applications we *do* consider is that they must be created and operated within limited dollar resources (in contrast to, for example, some one-of-a-kind military command-and-control systems). For these reasons, some readers may view this book as conservative; but we are firm in our belief that, although the data processing industry is one of the most rapidly moving technology-based industries, the *pace* at which it is moving is slowing, and that anything that is not already in (or is not presently entering) the technological repertoire will have little, if any, impact on the mainstream of data processing in the 1980-1985 period.

This book does not deal with most of the so-called "leading-edge" technological developments. Other topics that are not treated, or that are treated only superficially, include, among others:

- process control applications;
- manufacturing automation;
- computer-aided instruction;
- very large, one-of-a-kind applications such as military command-and-control or weather prediction;
- information retrieval (in the sense of library automation);
- research efforts in, for example, artificial intelligence, image and pattern processing, and self-teaching and heuristic systems.

We do not say a great deal about the *structure* of the data processing industry because we do not know how it is likely to change between now and 1985. We also do not explore very deeply the topic of *very* large data bases (distributed or otherwise) because very little is presently known about such data bases and their implications. Generally, we do not suggest *specific* solutions to the various problems that we enumerate; rather, we point out, where possible, some ways of searching for solutions. In some instances, we suggest which segment or segments of the industry might best do the searching.

Acknowledgements. The study that led to this book began in March, 1973, under the sponsorship of SHARE Inc. The recognition that such a study was needed grew out of discussions, in late 1972, between G. E. Gautney, Jr., then President of SHARE Inc., and T. E. Climis, then Vice President of IBM's System Development Division. Those discussions culminated in the generation of a large set of questions relating to the future of data processing and of the data processing industry during the period from 1980 to 1985. Seven SHARE Inc. participants—the authors of this book—were chosen to form a committee (known within SHARE Inc. as the SILT Committee, and chaired by the first author) to study these questions and problems.

We are grateful to SHARE Inc. for giving us the opportunity to participate in this effort. We think that we are wiser for having done so, and we encourage others to undertake similar efforts.

We thank our respective employers for the constant support they have given us in the form of resources and encouragement. We further thank, for their attention to detail and willingness to contribute, the many individuals, both within and outside SHARE Inc., who reviewed the various drafts of this book. The breadth and depth of their knowledge have contributed immensely to our efforts. We wish to emphasize, however, that none of these reviewers should be held responsible for any of the opinions expressed in this book; these opinions represent only the collective views of the authors.

Three individuals deserve specific acknowledgement for their help: J. F. Luke, of System Development Corporation, for his invaluable editorial assistance; J. F. Ossanna, of Bell Laboratories, who wrote the basic program used to typeset this book; and V. J. Fortney, also of Bell Laboratories, for verifying the accuracy of all the references in this book and for tracking down copies of a large number of hard-to-find reports, papers, etc.

A Note about Design and Typography. This book was designed and set in type in its entirety by the first author. Thus, the blame for all typographical errors, as well as for all mistakes of design, layout, etc., belongs to him, and not to the publisher.

Disclaimer. This book was written by the members of the SILT Committee of SHARE Inc. The views expressed in it are the majority views of that Committee. They do not necessarily represent the particular views of any of the corporations by whom any of the authors is employed.

March 1976

CONTENTS

DATA PROCESSING IN
1980-1985

1

OVERVIEW

*Had I been present at the creation, I
would have given some useful hints for
the better ordering of the universe.*
        Attr. to Alfonso X (the Wise)

This study explores the growth potential of the data processing
industry, extrapolates the expected developments in data processing
technology and practice, determines the developments required to
realize this potential, and identifies the areas in which requirements
exceed expectations. We examine, in detail, the gaps between the
needed capabilities and the capabilities that appear to be emerging, and
we identify changes in the emphasis and direction of data processing
research and development that are essential to bridge these gaps.
Finally, we recommend steps that we believe must be taken by the
data processing industry if its potential is to be realized. The reader
should keep in mind that this study is strongly, although by no means
exclusively, concerned with data processing in the United States.

The term "data processing industry," wherever used in this study,
includes all who are involved in providing data processing capabilities:
equipment and software manufacturers, programming and operations
staffs of user installations, professional organizations in data processing,
and university computer science departments.

The time period chosen for this study is 1980-1985. Two reasons
dictate this interval. First, it lies sufficiently far in the future to permit
concentration on broadly significant problems, unencumbered by
undue preoccupation with the serious but essentially transient
difficulties faced by data processing practitioners in their current day-
to-day work. Second, it is in general true that a minimum of five to ten

years is needed to bring a technological innovation from initial laboratory demonstration to general availability in practical applications[1]
[Bright 1973]. Thus, the results of research and development initiated
on the basis of our recommendations cannot be expected to have a
major impact until the 1980-1985 time period.

1. OVERVIEW OF THE BOOK

In successive chapters, we focus on:

- the external environment (Chapter 2);
- the users of data processing services (Chapter 3);
- the spectrum of data processing applications (Chapter 4);
- the future of hardware (Chapter 5);
- the future of software (Chapter 6);
- management and administrative concerns (Chapter 7).

Chapter 8 summarizes our conclusions and recommendations.

1.1. Environment

Examination of the environment is essential in order to determine the
context in which data processing must operate in the next two decades.
The environment will exert strong pressures on the data processing
industry, especially with respect to applications requirements, management needs, and availability of research resources. For this reason, an
explicit description and a forecast of the relevant environmental parameters are necessary.

"Environment" in our context means far more than simply physical
surroundings. For our purposes, the social, economic, and political
environments are the most critical. We have attempted to bound the
environmental variables in a manner that seems plausible. Certain
scenarios that we find implausible—worldwide adoption of a "back to
nature" philosophy, for example—could radically change the pressures
on the data processing industry, thereby invalidating some of our
conclusions.

The need to examine the environment for the period 1985-1995,
which is one decade beyond the technological horizon of our study,
follows from two obvious facts of contemporary practice:

---

1. This concept is sometimes called the "seven-year rule."

1. In-place systems have a non-zero life-span and, therefore, must have the capacity to satisfy user requirements for several years following their installation.

2. Many, if not most, installations prefer *not* to be on the "leading edge" of the data processing field, and are therefore satisfying their current needs with technology and techniques as much as ten years old. As evidence of this, we observe that there still exist today both sellers and buyers of used IBM 7080's, 1401's, etc.

The point is that, whether we like it or not, the applications systems that will be used for the remainder of the 1970's are being implemented *now*. If the "seven-year rule" alluded to above concerning the lag between conception and product availability is valid, then whatever influence this study may have will first affect applications systems being built in 1980-1985 for use in the period 1985-1995. Accordingly, Chapter 2 identifies reasonable bounds for the relevant environmental parameters that will condition information processing *needs* during the period 1980-1995.

Data processing has grown to the point where major social, business, and governmental functions are totally dependent upon it. In many cases, there is no possibility of reversion to manual procedures. The extent of current societal dependence on data processing can be appreciated from the fact that the use of computers was exempted from the order to reduce power consumption in Japan during the 1974 energy crisis [Upton 1974]. This dependence, as well as other factors *external* to the data processing industry, define what we mean by "environment." The environment will control the rate and direction of growth of the data processing industry, as well as the acceptance of its products and services.

It is not possible to explore all potential variations in the environment. Therefore, the environmental events that we forecast are essentially "surprise-free." We do not make allowance for a major war, which would, in all probability, radically alter the use of data processing resources and redirect data processing research. Neither do we make allowance for environmental, social, or political collapse in any of the major nations. We forecast the continued dominance of the presently developed nations, their emergence into "post-industrial" societies with the attendant growth in service industries, and the continued doubling of the overall dollar volume of the data processing industry every five years.

   Great care must be taken in making and using a forecast of the
kind attempted here; von Foerster, Mora, and Amiot [1960] provide an
illustration of how plausible assumptions and impeccable mathematics
can lead to unlikely conclusions (theirs is that world population
becomes infinite early in the next century; see also Serrin [1975]). We
believe we have avoided the errors of which they warn. We hope that
our forecast will be taken seriously, but we neither expect nor wish it
to be taken literally.

1.2. Users

The *sole* mission of the data processing industry is to provide data processing services to *end users*. In order to project the future of data processing, one must understand the needs and the characteristics of the
end users of data processing services. End users may interface with
data processing systems either directly (e.g., via terminals) or indirectly
(e.g., through clerks), but, in either case, their expectations and needs
must be understood by those who provide them with data processing
services.

   Within the data processing industry, there are other groups of individuals with different requirements. We define as *mid users* those
responsible for interpreting the end users' needs and translating them
into data processing services; in other words, the mid users are the data
processing professionals currently called "analysts" and "applications
programmers."

   Those who, in turn, satisfy the mid users' needs are the *system support users*. The system support users are the data processing
professionals who insulate the mid users from the complex collection
of hardware and software that constitutes the data processing system
itself. These users are also responsible for optimizing the resources
available within the system. The mid users and the system support
users utilize the system's capabilities to deliver data processing services
to the end users by means of data processing application programs. In
an attempt at relieving some of the problems associated with this task,
we introduce the concept of an Installation Control Program (ICP) to
act as an interface between the application programs and the System
Control Program (SCP) or Operating System (OS).

1.3. Applications

It is through the examination of the changes over time in the characteristics of data processing applications that one may understand most

clearly the direction of evolution of data processing. It proceeds from the environment of the 1950's, when the end users wrote and maintained their own application programs, to an environment where, today, the end users are dependent upon the services of large staffs of data processing professionals for the generation and maintenance of data processing applications. Applications are expanding throughout all levels of the typical enterprise, and there is an increasing emphasis upon the integration of many applications into a coherent, "total enterprise" set. Data processing will be more and more directly involved in the decision-making process; because of this, there will be increasing pressures to develop applications that capture data[2] in "real time" and that support the end users and other applications on a demand basis. We see no external constraint that will limit the expansion of requirements for "real-time" data processing services.

1.4. Hardware

The history of data processing hardware has been one of continual technological improvement that has resulted in increased capability in terms of speed, capacity, and sophistication. The dramatic improvements in the cost/performance ratio (in terms of the cost of instructions executed or bytes stored) will continue, although not at a uniform rate for all hardware components of data processing systems.

One result of business's growing dependence on data processing for its operation will be an increasingly stringent demand for *reliability* and *availability* of data processing capabilities. Hardware reliability will improve because of the inherent characteristics of the technology, architectural changes, and increased sophistication of the maintenance process. Emphasis will be on the availability of the *entire* data processing system. We anticipate that installations will assign a significantly higher priority to reliability and availability; this shift in priority will, in turn, provide economic justification for hardware solutions to the problem of system availability. These solutions will, of course, place additional stress on software support.

Just as the requirements and characteristics of applications will provide the emphasis needed for hardware solutions to problems of reliability and availability, data-base applications will force dramatic growth in capabilities of on-line storage. Likewise, the need for real-time

---

2. We observe that much of what we here call "data" consists in actuality of *decisions* or *proposals*. In other words, much "data" is derived from other steps in the decision-making process.

communications will force improvements in teleprocessing, from controllers to common-carrier facilities to terminals. Demand for applications that require distributed "intelligence" and distributed data will result in improved solutions to the problems of interconnecting computers.

Hardware evolution will change the relative costs attributable to various aspects of hardware. On the whole, total hardware costs in an installation will *not* decrease significantly, because the growth in the variety and size of applications will require more hardware, and because some of the potential decrease in the cost of hardware will be counterbalanced by attempts to make that hardware more reliable. The proportion of hardware expenditures devoted to particular components will shift, however. Teleprocessing expenditures, for instance, will increase over the period of our forecast. Overall, the *fraction* of the total data processing dollar spent on hardware will continue its downward trend. The proportion of the data processing dollar spent on software development will, in turn, continue its upward trend, thus increasing its preeminence as the most significant data processing expense.

Our technological forecast is conservative; it is concerned primarily with the estimation of hardware technology that will be *generally available* by 1985, rather than with potential "breakthroughs" that may not see broad acceptance until a later time. There will undoubtedly exist some "leading-edge" systems that will make our predictions seem timid, but they will not significantly affect the conclusions of this study.

It should also be emphasized that the major problems identified in this study are and will remain insensitive to details of system architecture. Such goals as quality, reliability, and manageability may be pursued with a variety of technological alternatives, but the underlying, fundamental requirement for significant improvement in these characteristics is independent of whether data processing systems consist of complexes of minicomputers or are huge, monolithic processors.

1.5. Software

Pressure upon the data processing industry to further exploit the opportunities inherent in the availability of data processing services results primarily in a demand for increases in the "inventory" of applications software.[3] Unfortunately, the growth of the industry to date

---

3. Throughout this book, we use the term "software" to denote *all* programs, including application programs, rather than just the so-called "systems software."

has not been primarily the result of an increase in the productivity of individual programmers, but rather a consequence of adding thousands of programmers to the data processing staffs. This historical solution of the need for increased applications development cannot continue successfully. The increasing interaction between applications means that the work of each programmer increasingly interacts with the work of other programmers, so that the demands for communication between programmers will tend to reduce individual output.

Early programs were relatively straightforward; programs written for an end user by a computer professional were the result of a very close one-to-one relationship between the programmer and the end user (who often were the same person). As data processing professionals became more numerous and more and more specialized, the average level of knowledge of data processing details decreased among the end users, while the knowledge of details of the various end users' areas of specialty decreased among the data processing professionals.

Today, an applications programmer, perhaps in combination with a system analyst, still solves the problems of creating the set of computer programs that ultimately result in a product that benefits the end user. The processes by which an applications programmer creates these programs today are fraught with opportunities for misunderstandings and errors that may or may not be detected. Initially, the programmer faces the problem of not even speaking the same language as the end user. The data processing professional must first surmount this barrier before he can understand the requirements of the end user and begin to produce an application that effectively supports that end user's needs. The lack of common understanding results in poor mechanisms for making trade-off decisions during the design of an application, as well as in a poor understanding of the penalties attendant on some of the choices. The result is a history, to date, of applications development cycles that are too long, too costly, and produce inadequate end products.

Concerns about productivity have tended to emphasize the productivity of the mid user, and, as the demand for applications increased, there have evolved tools for the mid user (such as higher-level languages) that were intended to trade the expertise of the programmer for machine capacity. A further evolution was the creation of the System Control Program (SCP), which performs the functions commonly required by a broad range of application programs. Therefore, it too is a productivity tool with respect to the applications programmer, since there is no longer any need to duplicate those programs that are already available in the SCP. Further, the applications programmer is relieved of the burden of interfacing directly with the hardware as a result of the SCP's having assumed that task.

The process that a programmer follows in developing an application has evolved by trial and error. Although most programmers are convinced that it works, it is a poorly understood process. Questions as to whether these techniques are optimum have not been answered adequately, nor is there a good understanding of the reasons for the failure of other techniques. It is only recently that ordered approaches to the applications development process, such as structured programming, have been proposed.

Even with these recent developments, programming and program design remain a craft. We began our work on this study with the collectively held optimistic view that the development of a *science* of computer programming was possible, desirable, and likely. We have not changed our opinion on the desirability of such a development, but we are now convinced, as a result of our study, that the lion's share of programming practice will remain a craft, at least within the time period considered here. One consequence of this conclusion is that the principal cost of software development will remain that of labor.

1.6. Management

If the potential benefits of data processing are to be realized, the most important changes required over the next decade will be those of management's approach to data processing. Historically, data processing entered most enterprises via administrative functions, and most data processing organizations probably still report to the controller. There are, of course, exceptions: research and engineering departments that tend to rely on data processing applications, and specialized applications, such as airline reservations systems, that have served to introduce data processing into the enterprise through other departments. Today, however, there tend to exist pressures, principally motivated by cost-saving efforts, to consolidate most of the data processing activities of an enterprise. We expect that this trend will continue into the future, along with a continued belief in the economy of scale.

As enterprises begin to understand the value of their corporate data as assets, many questions will arise regarding custody of, and access to, these assets. It is doubtful that questions regarding access to data can be resolved by the data processing departments alone; other elements of management associated with the data itself will be involved.

A data processing manager faces an increasingly complex world: there are problems of dealing with the vendors, who are offering increasingly broad lines of increasingly complex products in a world of rapid changes; there are changes in corporate policies and practices of the vendors, and of the manager's own enterprise; there are problems of changes in technology; and, on a continuing basis, data processing personnel must be trained, have their skills kept up to date, and be evaluated. For data processing to provide benefits to end users, it needs to be viewed as an integral part of the enterprise, receiving direct management support from other organizational entities, and responding to changes in the enterprise and in the emphasis of the business.

2. PREVIEW OF THE CONCLUSIONS

Our main conclusions are that, over the next decade, the major tasks of the data processing industry will be to improve:

- the quality of data processing services as perceived by the end users of these services;
- the resulting productivity of these end users; and
- the productivity of data processing systems and of data processing applications development efforts.

These improvements will have to be significantly larger than what would be achieved owing only to the passage of time.

It is worth noting some of the differences between the conclusions we have reached here and a corresponding set of conclusions that might have been arrived at by a similar study ten years ago:

- Hardware costs no longer are the major component of data processing expenditures; software costs are. Therefore, the cost-effectiveness of hardware is no longer the crucial concern that it once was.
- The data processing community no longer believes that there is magic in higher-level languages, or in operating systems, or in many other fads from the past, but it still continues to create new fads and calls *them* magic.
- The data processing community is coming to the realization that the software development craft is just that: a craft. It has a long way to go to become an engineering-like discipline, and even further to become a science; it is not clear that it will ever become a science.

- The data processing community has begun to worry a great deal (and rightly so) about the quality of the systems it builds.
- Data processing end users can no longer afford disruption of day-to-day data processing services: too much depends on these services. The same is true of the industry's growth: it could not, today, withstand the sort of disruption that was caused by conversion to third-generation systems in the mid 1960's.
- The entire national economy is vitally dependent on the availability of data processing. The pervasiveness of data processing is already very great. This was not so ten years ago. Ten years from now, society may well be *totally* dependent on data processing for its survival. Thus, the data processing industry has become, in the last ten years, a critical national resource, and will become more crucial every year from now on.

This study consists, in part, of a conventional forecast in the sense that the predicted socioeconomic and political developments, as well as the anticipated applications, are those that we *expect to occur*. The same is true of our technological forecast. In general, and especially in the hardware forecast, we have maintained a conservative view in order to be consistent with our objective of considering the mainstream of data processing development, as opposed to "leading-edge" activities.

The rest of our study is more in the fashion of a normative analysis, indicating what *should occur* in order to optimize the achievement of the expected applications. We recognize the feedback between applications requirements and available technology, and the fact that there is some synergy between needs and means, but we have chosen the view that the technology *can* be made available, and therefore we assume its existence in evaluating the spectrum of possibilities.

REFERENCES

Bright, J. R. 1973. The process of technological innovation. In *A guide to practical technological forecasting*, eds. J. R. Bright and M. E. F. Schoeman, pp. 3-12. Englewood Cliffs, NJ: Prentice-Hall.

Serrin, J. 1975. Is "Doomsday" on target? *Science* **189**:86-88.

Upton, M. 1974. Japan exempts DP from energy cutbacks. *Computerworld* **8**(7):27 (February 13).

von Foerster, H., Mora, P. M., and Amiot, L. W. 1960. Doomsday: Friday, 13 November, A.D. 2026. *Science* **132**:1291-95.

2

ENVIRONMENT

Columbus didn't just sail, he sailed west,
and the new world took shape from this
simple and, we now think, sensible design.
E. B. White

1. INTRODUCTION

This chapter presents what we consider to be a likely scenario for the course of political, economic, and social events during the period from now until 1985. We present an economic projection that is internally consistent and "surprise-free" in the sense of Kahn and Bruce-Briggs [1972], in that we will not be surprised if actual developments parallel the projection. Although it has many of the characteristics of a naive economic model, this projection is broader, more sophisticated, and, therefore, more useful. It is described as if it were exact—in the sense that no indication of probable error is given—although we clearly do not expect that, for example, the Gross National Product (GNP) of the United States will be *precisely* 1.97 trillion dollars in 1985 (see Table A.2 in Appendix A).

Time has not permitted us to explore any of the possible variances, either through sensitivity analyses or through the construction of less likely scenarios. For our purposes, it will make little difference whether the details of the projection are in error; we believe that the *general trends* will hold and that the trends, not the details, are important.

This analysis has been carried out in the spirit of the relatively new discipline of policy research, which relies on forcing an objective analysis of trends by abstracting and mathematizing everything possible. It has the positive value of suppressing hopes (or fears), but at the same time has the danger of overlooking profound implications. It is far from perfect, and the methodologies vary substantially [Dickson 1971, chap. 11], but we believe it to be the best of the alternatives available to us. The quantitative basis for this analysis is found in the appendices.

We have attempted to be precise about what we mean. Whether the projection we present is better or worse than the imaginable, attainable alternatives is left to the judgment of the reader. A detailed analysis of the theoretical basis for such studies can be found in de Jouvenel [1967].

Five major assumptions have guided the construction of this projection. They are that there will be:

1. *No major war.* For a war to count as "major," there must be a real potential for the use of nuclear weapons. The Middle East will, in all likelihood, continue to be an area of armed conflict for some time in the future, but so long as NATO and the Warsaw Pact countries stand aside, and so long as nuclear weapons are not used, such a conflict is not to be considered "major." A military venture comparable to the recent war in Indochina would perturb but not invalidate this assumption.

2. *No uncontrollable economic dislocation in industrialized countries.* The kind of economic dislocation to which this assumption refers is that for which the modern archetype is the period 1929-1939. Certainly no economic event since the commencement of the Marshall Plan would indicate failure of this assumption. Minor dislocations that may be painful to those involved, but that do not significantly interrupt the long-term trends, are both expected and irrelevant.[1] The figures presented in Appendix A are based on sufficiently long-term trend lines and stabilized data to be insensitive to the inflationary dislocations and normal business cycles characteristic of the post-World War II global environment, provided that they are correctly interpreted as indicating the measure of *long-term* trends, and *not* as explicit predictions for specific years.

---

1. The "energy crisis" is an example of this kind of phenomenon, at present sufficiently moderate in impact to only perturb, not demolish, economic stability [Pollack 1974]. This situation, however, could clearly become sufficiently destabilizing to bring about worldwide depression, substantial restructuring of many institutions, and invalidation of the trend predictions made here. Furthermore, the shortage of energy is just an example, recently realized, of the critical dependence of economic health on resource availability.

3. *No political revolution in a major country.* We assume here that "revolution" means what it says. An internal Kremlin power struggle or the constitutional impeachment of a U.S. President would not count. An event comparable to President Allende's ouster in Chile, were it to occur in a major country (e.g., in the United States or in the United Kingdom), *might* change the ground rules for world behavior sufficiently to invalidate some part of the subsequent analysis.

4. *No epochal social revolution.* "Social revolution" is a difficult term to define precisely. In some sense, the entire twentieth century can be viewed as a time of continuing social revolution. However, if we take today's pace of social change as the norm, then "social revolution" in the *current* context must mean the consequences of an event that is both extremely rapid and highly dramatic. In his time, Martin Luther counted; in ours, the contemporary counterculture does not.

5. *No epistemological revolution.* This assumption requires some explanation. It is perhaps most easily understood if we give some examples of phenomena that would cause it to be violated. These might include: discovery that the speed of light is not a universal limit; invention of a practical matter duplicator; development of reliable telepathy; proof of the existence of extraterrestrial intelligence; and, most importantly, the totally unexpected. Comparable historical events are the successful return of Columbus, the Copernican Revolution, the invention of the Arabic number system, and Einstein's formulation of the theory of relativity. On this issue of epistemology, cause and effect are extremely difficult to disentangle, and what seems trivial can have enormous historical consequences. For instance, it can be persuasively argued that the introduction of the horse collar into Europe in the thirteenth century [Singer et al. 1956] signaled the demise of Feudalism and thus led to the American, French, and Russian revolutions, and, thereby, to the modern world. We simply postulate that the current scientific world view will not be radically altered in the next two decades.

Not all the authors of this study are equally persuaded by the projection methodology adapted from Kahn and his colleagues. However, the general trends deduced are not in dispute, and many of the variables can change in value *either way* without altering the consequences for the data processing industry. As an example, a plenitude of energy will lead to increased concern for ecology, resulting in many new data processing applications. On the other hand, a shortage of energy may suppress ecological concerns but will stimulate data processing applications in the areas of energy conservation, development, and distribution. Although the applications may change, the *amount* of data processing is not likely to change greatly.

Given these assumptions, which can be summarized as military, economic, political, social, and epistemological stability, a projection for the next twenty years can be constructed that results in, at least, a recognizable world. The data displayed in Appendix A indicate the major economic parameters of this projection.

Two major economic trends are apparent from the data. First, the world is sharply dichotomized in economic strength between the developed and underdeveloped countries. Twenty percent of the world's population enjoys eighty percent of its wealth, and the disparity (on a GNP-per-capita basis) is getting larger, not smaller (see Table A.3 of Appendix A). Furthermore, only the developed countries have the surplus resources to invest in high-technology enterprises like data processing systems. For the rest of this century, at least, the lion's share of the data processing "action" is going to remain where it has been up to now: North America, Europe, the USSR, Japan, and Australia.[2]

The second trend is less well known but equally valid and more pertinent to the present issues; it concerns the entry, during the time span we are considering, of the developed nations into the socio-economic category increasingly called "post-industrial society"—a category that we believe the United States has already entered. The precise definitions vary, but a rough indicator is a per capita GNP in excess of 4,000 to 4,500 (1970 U.S.) dollars. Not all experts agree on whether this is a truly meaningful criterion, or on whether it has in fact already occurred in the United States, but most do agree that significant changes are in process [Bell 1973]. The principal characteristics of a post-industrial society are summarized by Kahn and Wiener [1967], from whom the following are derived:

- Economic activities are service oriented rather than production oriented.
- Urbanization and the trend toward megalopolis continue.
- An income "floor" is established.

---

2. We do not expect this conclusion to be disturbed by the current influx of oil revenues into the Arab world.

- Efficiency per se is no longer primary.
- There is widespread "cybernation."
- "National interest" values are eroded.
- "Work ethic" is eroded.
- Knowledge industry is paramount.
- Culture is sensate, secular, and humanist.

All of these observations bear on the nature, diversity, and acceptance of future information processing systems [Dantzig and Saaty 1973]. Indeed, we believe that these socioeconomic changes would force the invention of large, data-base oriented information processing systems if such systems had not already been invented. The pressure to use, expand, and improve these systems has already become enormous and irresistible, despite the known and feared undesirable side effects of the widespread installation of systems providing rapid, complete, and unregulated access to stored data. In making this observation, we disagree somewhat with the assertion of Westin and Baker [1972] that there is relatively little danger inherent in the *present* situation; in any case, we strongly agree with their thesis that *now* is the time to take precautions against future misuses of data banks.

This chapter does not deal with issues of privacy and freedom except to observe that if our conclusions are valid, these issues are even more important than they have yet been assumed to be. We note also that there is a great likelihood of regulation in this area, and that much of it will be ill-conceived. We view privacy as a political problem, about which all citizens should be concerned. Data processing professionals cannot claim superior validity for their views on what should be kept private. However, we can and do discuss the *technical* problems of implementing whatever privacy decisions are made by legislative or regulatory bodies. Where privacy involves data or system security, professionals have a duty as experts to bring to the appropriate forums their knowledge of what is and is not technically feasible, and at what price.

2. LEGAL, REGULATORY, AND STANDARDIZATION ISSUES

One of the characteristics of post-industrial society is the emergence of a regulated economy. The early examples of regulation in the United States, such as the Sherman and Clayton Acts, were defensive in nature, tending to protect the public against rapacious use of monopolistic economic power. More recently, the law and various administrative regulations have been used in attempts to achieve economic and social optimization; however, human nature and the political process combine to guarantee disagreement on what counts as optimum. Nevertheless, the trend is clear and unmistakable: regulation is going to be the way of life.

The effect of this trend on the data processing industry is twofold. First, within the industry itself, the posture of the vendors is difficult to assess in view of the unresolved conflicts between the "mainframe" vendors and the suppliers of "pluggable" units (both hardware and software); between the equipment manufacturers and the middlemen such as leasing companies; between IBM and the U.S. Justice Department; and between the government and everyone else in such areas as standards. Not all of these issues will be fully resolved by 1985. Second, the industry will be more and more subject to regulation of data processing applications themselves. The first serious instance of such regulatory authority will be in the area of data banks. A data privacy act has already been passed in Sweden [Bloor 1974], proposed legislation has been read in the British Parliament, and the U.S. Congress has enacted the Privacy Act of 1974 (5USC552a) concerning privacy in the Federal Government and has under consideration H.R.1984, which extends this legislation to the private sector. Additional legislation at the state level has been passed, and more is a certainty in the next decade.

Fraudulent behavior, such as that turned up in the Equity Funding scandal [Robertson 1973], has brought calls for more stringent regulation of financial data processing applications, without much regard for the fact that there is really no way in which a data processing system can be protected against the introduction of realistic but false data by one or more authorized users.

While calls for immediate certification of programmers and programs may offend the sensibilities of some responsible professionals, and while there is no evidence that such certification is beneficial to anyone, there are clear indications that many, both within and outside the data processing industry, feel that there is a need for some action in this area.

Various studies of regulatory agencies and regulated industries suggest two effects one can expect from increased application of government regulation to a previously open and unregulated business. First, in contrast to conventional social theory, such regulation tends to drive out the small entrepreneur. Second, regulation makes everything in the business more expensive. A fair estimate is that cost figures based on today's environment should be inflated by 10% to take regulation into account.

Another phenomenon that will affect the data processing industry will result from the growth of regulatory activities in *other* industries. This will increase the need for data processing facilities in these industries. A significant portion of the 10% loss of effectiveness caused by the regulation of an industry is due to the cost of additional data processing facilities needed to satisfy the record-keeping and reporting requirements of the regulatory bureaucracy. A recent example of the problem is the requirement for allocation control imposed on heating-oil suppliers.

In addition to the data processing facilities required to first supply the information needed for effective regulation and to then evaluate this information to ensure compliance, it will be necessary to do extensive modeling, both to evaluate the consequences of existing regulations and to explore the potential impact of proposed regulation.

Beyond simply adding to the applications load, the imposition of regulation will cause a great deal of data interchange, which brings with it the need for interchange standards with respect both to physical media and to logical structure. The government already exerts pressure in this area, and the pressure will get more intense. This is an area in which the data processing industry can help itself if it can generate the will to do so. But the industry as a whole should participate, rather than leaving the field to the government and to the vendors.

Of course, there are a variety of technical and economic reasons for development and use of standards other than protection from government imposition. The increase in scope and complexity of data processing applications and the associated, apparently exponential, growth in cost and difficulty of their successful implementation can be mitigated, to some extent, through the timely development of data processing industry standards.

Both national and international standards are needed in areas such as data elements, communications formats, human interface languages, and the like [ANSI 1973]. Studies already underway may suggest other areas in which standardization is needed. It will be vital to successful implementation of large, integrated, distributed systems to have such standards well thought out *in advance* of applications system design. Thus, what is really needed are *systems* of standards, adequately integrated to permit the orderly development of large and complex data processing systems, allowing systematic replacement of both hardware and software components without disruption. The industry generally will default on its obligations (and fail to look after its own needs) if it defers, without thought, to the government in the development of standards. At the moment, it is left almost entirely to the vendors to defend the needs of the data processing industry and its users.

Care must be taken in the development of standards to ensure that immediate gains are not obtained at the expense of long-term losses. Standards that constrain *how* equipment is made or a process performed should *not* be developed. This approach generally has the effect of limiting the use of existing technology, as well as limiting technological innovation by undermining the clever inventor. Standards should, rather, be concerned with interfaces between system components. As an obvious example, standard magnetic tape recording formats are sensible, but standard *compilers* for programming languages would not be appropriate. Refining this position needs definition and study.

A legal problem of potentially major significance that has hardly been attacked at all is the question of liability for system failure. It is difficult enough in today's environment to identify the reason for a failure when the only *real* pressure is to decide who can fix the problem. In complex, on-line systems composed of both hardware and software units provided by a number of suppliers, and where the "operator" of the system suffers exposure to legal action in the event of a failure, the question of liability becomes far more critical. It will become essential for contracts to specifically assign liability and for system design to facilitate the identification of such responsibility.

The possibility of a legal requirement to capitalize the cost of software development (as opposed to treating it as a current expense item) has a potential and, as yet, not fully analyzed impact on data processing departments. Traditionally, capitalization has often made it difficult to "sell" projects to higher management, sometimes simply because it raises the management level at which such decisions can be made. Also, capitalization often forces calculations of return on investment to be made with much more precision and care than has been typical for software projects, and it certainly affects the "make-versus-buy-versus-lease" decisions. It has been observed that, in the case of new technological developments, business managements tend to act as if the cost of capital were significantly higher than it actually is [Linstone 1974].

Another legal issue that affects the data processing industry is the protection of software. This area is quite murky at the moment, but no matter how it clears up eventually, it seems unlikely to have a major impact, provided care is taken in framing legislation so that the incentive to innovate is preserved, such incentive being, fortunately, a well-understood principle in this area of the law. Legislation may alter to some degree the *way* in which programs are sold or leased, but it cannot seriously affect *what* programs are sold or leased, or affect their cost in a way that truly matters. For a detailed examination of these legal issues, see COSATI [1973].

3. ECONOMIC ISSUES

By examining Tables A.4 through A.6 of Appendix A in some detail, one can infer that productivity increases in the traditional primary and secondary industries (agriculture, mining, manufacturing) are possible through the mechanisms of conventional automation. The problem of attaining these increases arises in the tertiary and quaternary industries (transportation, trade, finance, services, and government), as well as in the management and marketing functions of the primary and secondary industries; conventional automation provides some help with this problem, but hardly enough to achieve productivity increases (over 1975) by a factor of 1.38 in 1985 and a factor of 1.89 in 1995, as postulated in the "GNP per man-year" line of Table A.4. These increases can come only, so far as existing technology suggests, from organization, concentration, and effective resource management, which implies information availability and, therefore, data-base oriented systems [Nolan 1973]. Indeed, about 60% of the applications discussed in the GUIDE/IBM Delphi Study [Wylie 1971] imply the widespread existence of data-base oriented systems.

The shock effect of very widespread introduction of data processing into the purview of the general public may be lessened by the potential appearance of computers in the home (see Section 5 of Chapter 4). If home computers become widespread, large numbers of people will become familiar with data processing in a congenial environment and will, as a result, be less apt to recoil from other encounters with data processing.

The erosion of "national interest" values and of the economic independence of individual nations is evidenced by the continued growth of multinational corporations. More and more of the economic activity of the world is being conducted by enterprises that are multi-national in scope and outlook. Perlmutter [1971] notes that, by the 1980's, "a unitary global industrial-commercial system, a worldwide network of industrial, financial and commercial activities . . . could produce 50 to 75 percent of the gross . . . product of the world. The key participants are likely to be 200 to 400 supergiant corporations doing a billion to 160 billion dollars (each) of annual sales." This observation is supported by a simple extrapolation of today's figures, which show the multinationals with 15% of the gross world product, and a collective growth rate of 10% per annum.

This discussion is not intended to imply that the world will become less belligerent and more internationalist by 1985. It does, however, reflect our assumption that there will be no major war; and beyond that, it suggests that the world is becoming highly integrated in an economic sense and that the business community is currently tending toward the view that self-interest is best served not by jingoism, but by an internationalist point of view.

It should be noted here that, at the moment, there are very few, if any, mechanisms for effectively regulating the behavior of multi-national corporations. Indeed, pressures for increased and free trade, especially the growth of trade between Western and Eastern countries, tend to act against the establishment of such regulatory mechanisms. Nevertheless, there is increasing public concern over the problem of uncontrolled actions by multinational corporations, and the U.S. Congress is beginning to talk about it. Complicating the picture are the increase in the number of countries in which multinational corporations have their home bases, the multigovernmental economic units such as the European Economic Community (EEC) and the Organization of Petroleum Exporting Countries (OPEC), and the Japanese economic structure where the entire economy of the country acts much like a multinational conglomerate [Kahn 1970].

4. SOCIETAL ISSUES

Several quite fundamental societal problems obtrude in a way that suggests serious impact on the U.S. data processing industry, despite the assumption of fundamental social stability. They fall, very broadly, into four basic categories:

1. erosion of the "work ethic";

2. increase in the rate of social change;

3. possibility of collapse of the U.S. system of higher education;

4. imposition of ecological constraints.

Each of these points is defined and elaborated upon below.

4.1. Work Ethic and Automation

The concept of salvation through work is, of course, relatively modern. In all civilizations prior to the advent of Western Christendom during the seventh and eighth centuries, most "work" was done by slaves and by poorer citizens who could not afford slaves [de Grazia 1964]. Even Feudalism did not change things very much, the serf being only a slave with some well-defined rights. It was the "second generation" protestant theologians, such as Knox, Calvin, and Wesley, who promoted sloth to primacy as a sin. This study is not the place to explore the relationship between this philosophy and the onset of the industrial revolution, although we find it difficult to believe that there is no connection between the two.

However necessary the "work ethic" may have been to the growth of Western Christendom from a feudal economy, through industrialization, to today's mass consumption society (which is now on the brink of becoming post-industrial), it is at best atavistic in the context of industrialization and automation. If it takes almost nobody to make and distribute almost everything necessary or desirable to nearly everybody, why work?

In an industrial society, the counterparts of slaves and serfs were factory workers and manual laborers. Although their work tended to be tedious and not self-rewarding, it at least had tangible products: bolts of cloth from the mills, automobiles from the assembly lines, etc. In a post-industrial society, the perceived relationship between labor and product is more tenuous, and the tedium is compounded by the loss of a tangible sense of productiveness. The satisfaction of work is then practically nil. Increasingly, the clerical worker is the new "serf." When satisfaction is an increasingly important element of motivation to work (relative to material gain), its loss is a severe deterrent to the desire to work. To the extent that public assistance increases, the marginal increase in material gain becomes less relevant. It should be noted in this context that public assistance is not simply a temporarily popular manifestation of the socialist political theory. In the time of Julius Caesar, 20% of the population of Rome received public assistance in the form of free food, and, by the time of Augustus, it was 32% [Rostovtzeff 1927].

It is thus already difficult, and will become increasingly so in the near future, for teachers and preachers extolling the virtues of labor to capture and maintain the faith of the populace. Manifestations of this are not the communes and "doing your own thing," but rather labor's push for a shorter work week and the elimination of compulsory overtime. A few people, however motivated, living in the New Mexico desert, will not materially impact the next two decades, but a 15% reduction, on the average, in man-hours per worker certainly will.

The 15% figure just noted is the approximate result of granting all of organized labor's current demands. That will not happen overnight, but if past performance is any guide, it all will have been granted in ten years. The growth of the number of women in the labor force as a result of the collective set of phenomena known as "women's liberation" may counteract, for the next decade or two, the pattern of overall decline in the percentage of the population at work. The relevant conclusion for this study is that there will be demand for more productivity (measured by output per man-hour) and, therefore, for more automation.

A concomitant of this will be increased respectability of automation. If people do not plan to work anyway, there is little point in their denigrating the devices that permit them leisure. Indeed, the International Longshoremen's and Warehousemen's Union (ILWU) under Harry Bridges has negotiated contracts that permit an arbitrary degree of automation, provided that *present* ILWU members do not lose by it. This is almost certain to become the norm rather than the exception in the next fifteen years. This phenomenon will undoubtedly assist in improving the rather deplorable public image of data processing. As both the ubiquity and significance of data processing increase, we can expect improved understanding of the role of data processing and, hence, less tendency to blame "the computer" for human error.

4.2. Rate and Kind of Future Changes

The concept of "future shock" has been documented in a journalistic fashion by Toffler [1970]. While Toffler's picture is somewhat bizarre and overly dramatic, his observations appear to be sound, and our projection must take them into account. Simply stated, his argument is that the world is changing so rapidly that most people cannot cope with the rate of change, and that, furthermore, the rate of change is itself increasing.

The reality, of course, is that so long as enough people can and will cope, the phenomenon does not really matter in the long view, and that, when most people will no longer be able to cope, the rate of change will decrease. It *must* be a self-limiting process [Dunn 1971]. Sociologically, that is most interesting; from the point of view of our study, it is marginal, except for Toffler's observation about how people cope: he notes that the increase in the rate of change results in the development of individuals with loyalty to their profession, as opposed to their company. The aerospace industry was perhaps the first to experience this extensively; the data processing industry is now experiencing it to a great degree. The increasing trends toward apartment living, general citizen mobility, portable pensions, and other effects that permit individuals to establish personal, movable "cocoons" will reinforce this trend in many other industries. The effect of this pattern on industry generally is not well known, yet it may well be serious, especially in its impact on personnel turnover rates. It is worth noting that this phenomenon is most acutely present in professions that require a high degree of technical training, which are precisely the professions that are going to be most needed to run the coming, highly automated society.

Two recently recognized phenomena not reflected in the demographic and economic projections appearing in Appendix A are the trend toward zero population growth in the developed countries and the growing worldwide shortage of natural resources. A concomitant of zero population growth is a stabilization of the size of the labor force, which traditionally is one component of economic growth. With zero population growth, economic growth comes *only* from productivity gains. This increases the pressure on automation and data processing to contribute to productivity.

A consequence of worldwide shortages of some natural resources is the increased emphasis on the efficient use of available resources. This will cause substantial effort to be devoted to the development and improvement of data processing applications in the areas of process control and manufacturing control, as well as in the areas related to the preservation of the environment (see Section 4.4 below).

These two phenomena only serve to emphasize the critical importance of effective data processing growth to the health of the economy.

4.3. Educational Issues

Data processing is plagued by a lack of coupling between the research community and the practical world of applications. A great deal of research is done, but much of it, including a lot that should not, gets published and subsequently ignored. (The double entendre is deliberate: much of what gets published should not be published in the first place; on the other hand, much of what gets published gets, unfortunately, subsequently ignored. Possibly the former is partially responsible for the latter.) In a sense, this observation is a complaint that programming is still a craft or a "cottage industry." An engineering-like discipline is needed, based on the computer-science equivalent of basic physics; a science that has yet to be (and may never be) invented or discovered.

This situation is the fault of nearly everybody. Too many partially qualified individuals are accepted for graduate study in fields related to data processing. A large number of substandard theses are accepted; the resulting additions to faculties are consequently of uneven quality; the high caliber work that is produced is either misunderstood or ignored by industry; and industry generally criticizes in a carping, rather than constructive, manner. Taken literally, this charge may be too harsh, but each of these elements is present to a degree.

Related to the above point is the issue of the practical relevance of academic curricula. The typical computer science graduate may be trained to write clever compilers for both real and exotic languages and, perhaps, to prove theorems about the correctness of very short ALGOL 68 programs. Often the result appears to industry as analogous to preparing for a surgical career by concentrating on a study of molecular biochemistry. Of course, we fully recognize the importance of biochemistry to medicine, as well as the importance of mathematics to engineering and of compiler theory to computing, but we take issue with the relative emphasis and with the lack of attention to the development of engineering-like and management-like disciplines in data processing. In this area, the universities and the data processing professional societies are most at fault. Too much attention is paid to academic respectability, and not enough to the real need for the equivalent of an engineering discipline. The existence of 175,000 general-purpose data processing systems (and almost a million dedicated systems—see Table B.2 of Appendix B) will force a change; it remains to be seen whether it is accepted gracefully or swallowed painfully. We return briefly to this topic in Section 4.5 of Chapter 7.

A more general and more serious problem is the absence of responsible cooperation between society as a whole and the present academic structure. Universities used to enjoy esteem paralleling that of the churches; both seem to be toppling in the public image today. Public schools were once the avenue out of the ghetto or away from the immigration dock. Today, they tend to be battlegrounds for issues at best remotely related to education. Part of the problem—perhaps the major part—is the spiraling costs.

The figures given by the Association of American Universities [AAU 1973], if extrapolated into the next decade, lead to such absurdities in tuition costs that it is clear that some really drastic action is urgently needed. The AAU report advocates the need to maintain tax deductions for educational gifts. The case is moderately persuasive in terms of tax policies, but is grimly inadequate in terms of the obvious needs. It is abundantly evident that, if industry wants a continuing supply of young employees adequately educated by a process even remotely resembling the traditional higher-education system, then it is going to have to pay most of the bill, either directly or through increased taxation by central governments. Alternatives exist, the General Motors Technical Institute being one example. Whatever the solution, it must be found, or many of the needs presented in this study (as well as most other needs) will fail to be met for lack of implementors.

One alternative that could have an important impact on data processing is to return to the medieval concept of education: universities are for training prospective researchers and teachers, while practitioners learn their skills as apprentices, and the modern counterpart of the guild is a trade school. Certain professions are somewhat like that now. Despite formal association with universities, most law and medical schools are, in effect, trade schools. Should this approach be found useful for data processing, it has the significant advantage of being implementable by the industry, independently of a requirement to modify traditional higher education. This approach does, however, have the disadvantage of even further widening the gap between research and practice.

4.4. Ecological Issues

Although, in retrospect, environmental abuse has been a growing problem since the industrial revolution, events of the second half of the twentieth century have brought into the open the existence of ecological limits to mankind's expansion. The *direct* impact of this on data processing is, of course, minimal. Computers do not pollute, consume significant amounts of scarce resources, endanger species, or otherwise distort the environment in any obvious way. The misdirected charge that they permit other acts that despoil the environment is on a par with the complaint that computers per se are dehumanizing. To the extent that there is any validity to these charges, the fault obviously lies with the user and his chosen uses; and, parenthetically, therein lies a serious public education problem for the data processing industry.

The indirect consequences of these ecological considerations on the data processing industry are significant. One of the obvious effects is the use of data processing for pollution monitoring and control, analytical environmental impact studies, and ecological modeling. More important, but more difficult to analyze, is the potential contribution of data processing to overall technological growth. Recent studies [Meadows et al. 1972; Forrester 1971] have suggested that the future holds a serious degradation in the quality of life, no matter what mankind does in an attempt to prevent it. Responsible challenges to this thesis have appeared [Starr and Rudman 1973] on the grounds that the earlier studies have treated technological growth as constant or arithmetic in progression, while in reality it is geometric. A major factor in continued exponential technological growth is certain to be an expansion of information processing capability. Studies of the trade-offs between resource availability and quality of life will undoubtedly stimulate research and development in many areas of data processing, and, collectively, they may well do for data processing in the next decade what the space program did in the last. Conversely, efforts to protect the ecology may depend as heavily on data processing as did the space program.

5. REQUIREMENTS FOR DATA PROCESSING CAPABILITY

In addition to these relatively novel pressures for growth in data processing, there are also more conventional political and economic effects to consider. Pressures exist from several directions to extend and elaborate various kinds of government services. Some form of income floor, universal medical care (whether supplied, insured, or simply paid for by the government), natural-resource management, and expanded educational facilities are all but inevitable. They all require the availability of a wide variety of information that is capable of being accessed and processed with ease.

In order to manage the increased flow of money associated with general economic growth, and especially with the increased international integration of economies, a major restructuring of financial institutions is certain to occur. The volume of financial paper currently being moved around the world is already absurd, and its impending growth cannot be handled. The Monetary and Payments System Planning Committee of the American Bankers Association [ABA 1971] is moving toward a series of recommended actions that will, in effect, make the records activity of the entire banking system in North America (and ultimately in the world) into a single data base. The credit records assimilation activities, as reported in Westin and Baker [1972], go hand in hand with this bank activity.

Additional pressures for restructuring the financial industry are coming from several sources. The general ill health of securities markets around the world is one source; the public scrutiny under which U.S. commodities markets are coming, as a result of stark increases in food prices, is another; and, in an action that will affect essentially all major U.S. life insurance companies, New York State has recently granted permission to life insurance companies to sell "variable" life insurance, wherein the amount of claim paid is dependent on the investment success of the insurance company, thus effectively broadening the base of securities dealers.

All of this means a rapidly moving reorganization of the world's financial institutions. Much of this reorganization is going to be accomplished through the use of automation on a massive, international scale. With some exceptions, integrity of data and security of information will be the paramount considerations, rather than instant response. It should also be noted here that the observations about government regulation apply as strictly to the financial industry as to any other and, further, that the meaning of fraud is more obvious in this area of data processing applications.

These major trends will be supplemented by many other (only relatively less significant) activities implying high-performance, reliable data processing systems. The GUIDE/IBM Delphi Study [Wylie 1971] lists many such applications for the 1980-1985 period—indeed, far too many to itemize here. Perhaps the most significant enabling development assumed in that study is that, by 1985, the cost/performance of mass storage will improve by a factor of 1,000.

Another equally significant trend is the substantial data processing capability that is currently available at a relatively small (and still rapidly decreasing) cost through minicomputers. The potential impact of minicomputers is enormous, as outlined in Sections 4 and 5 of Chapter 4, and in Section 8 of Chapter 5.

Trends such as those suggested above have been widely discussed and strongly disputed, often on the grounds that there is insufficient money to pay for the implementation of all these ideas and that the data processing industry is maturing and reaching a plateau. In a world where large corporations seriously consider the cost-benefit trade-offs of private corporate communication satellites, the first objection is not, in our opinion, a very realistic one. As to the second, it should be recalled that there was a widespread belief in 1955 that all of the world's computing needs would be satisfied with thirty or forty IBM 704's. Regarding the required investment, Japan has a proposed program to accomplish much of what has been suggested here (and, in some directions, more) at a cumulative cost of 20 trillion yen (65 billion 1970 U.S. dollars). This program (Japan Computer Usage Development Institute [JCUDI 1972]) calls for less absolute annual outlay than the annual NASA budget during the APOLLO years. In terms of percent of GNP, of course, it is a substantial fraction, being, on the average, 0.47% of the Japanese GNP, in contrast to our estimate of 0.1% of the U.S. GNP devoted to data processing research (see Table B.7 of Appendix B).

It is not possible to do more than construct an order-of-magnitude estimate of the consequences of the explicit and implied spread of applications derivable from the above observations. Putting together all the data known to us, however, it is reasonable to expect that, in 1985, there will exist 175,000 distinct general-purpose data processing systems, excluding stand-alone minicomputers and other dedicated systems (distinct in the sense that they are independently useful and used), containing, in the aggregate, 10^{16} bytes of non-transient data. This represents more than a twofold multiplication in the number of major systems over today's base, and a thousand-fold increase in stored data. Most of those systems will be physically connectable with at least some others. A reasonable estimate of the cost of their establishment and operation is 164 billion dollars a year by 1985. The groundwork for these systems is being laid now. Appendix B contains the analysis leading to these estimates.

One final point of some significance to the overall growth of data processing is the estimated size of large data bases in the 1980's. Using the figures developed in Wylie [1971], *individual* data bases may be as large as 10^{12} bytes of non-transient data [Steel 1974]. This may be contrasted with the estimate of non-redundant data in the world's libraries in 1985 of 4×10^{14} bytes [Senders 1963].

6. PREREQUISITES TO GROWTH

The remainder of this chapter is concerned with some steps that must be taken, starting now, to minimize the difficulties that will be associated with the indicated developments. Five major points are considered:

1. management awareness;

2. information security;

3. vendor effectiveness;

4. research resources;

5. standards.

6.1. Management Awareness

First, corporate managers—all the way to the top—must become more aware of the implications and importance of data processing systems to the survival of their enterprises. Managers must also become far more aware than they are now that these systems are going to become central elements in the management control and operations of almost every large-scale undertaking. Ultimately, management must develop organizational structures that will permit effective utilization of data processing tools; we return to this topic in Section 4 of Chapter 7.

Managers do, of course, tend to ask disturbingly pertinent questions such as "How much will that cost?" and "What is its value to the company?" At the moment, responsible answers to such questions are not possible because adequate tools (such as measuring and monitoring devices, system models, data reduction and analysis procedures, reporting techniques) have not yet been perfected. Furthermore, there is feedback between tool definition and the identification of the kinds of questions that should be asked.

6.2. Information Security

Another issue that management must face is that of security. Appropriate measures for physical security are well understood, if not always practiced. Fire, flood, power loss, mad bombers, disgruntled employees, and simple frauds can, by and large, be held in check by conventional protection, prevention, and recovery mechanisms. Data processing and communications systems, however, involve another dimension of security—namely *information* protection. This is one subject about which much is known and very little published, primarily because its principal area of application has been government communications security, where everything pertinent is highly classified. Kahn [1967] provides a provocative glimpse behind this shroud of secrecy and gives some hint of the relevant considerations.

The need for information security has two sources: privacy considerations and commercial intelligence protection. While the motivation, ethical considerations, and regulatory legislation will be radically different on these points, the basic principles employed to achieve the necessary security are essentially the same. Encryption has been the preferred solution from the time of Julius Caesar to the present. Feistel [1973] discusses some current techniques applicable to data processing.

Two principles of information security need to be better understood. First, there is no such thing, in practice, as an "unbreakable code." There are theoretically unbreakable systems, but they must be used by people, and people make mistakes that can lead to lapses in security. The second principle derives in part from the first. One can get whatever degree of protection one wants (short of perfection) if one is willing to pay for it. The expectations of the thief, as well as the intrinsic value of the information to its owner, must guide the expenditure of security resources. Thus, the key to satisfactory information security is to determine the value of the information *to the potential unauthorized user,* as well as its intrinsic value to its legitimate owner, and then to design a security system that will make it more costly than the smaller of these two values to obtain the information without permission during the appropriate length of time.

Management is going to need an understanding of these principles, because it will no longer be the case that the principal tasks of the security officer are to see to adequate fire protection, to the guarding of the physical plant, and to other such conventional physical security measures. An approach involving the personnel, facilities, and procedures of the entire enterprise is necessary to provide true security, because the possibilities for compromise are widespread and often subtle. Furthermore, ensuring any real degree of security can be expensive. Without explicit examples to dissect, it is not possible to provide hard numbers, but appropriate protection of data bases containing highly sensitive information could increase the cost by as much as 30% [Steel 1974].

6.3. Vendor Effectiveness

Vendor effectiveness, in the sense of the ability of the vendor to supply needed, high-quality products that perform, without fault, as advertised, has been discussed universally and almost ad nauseam. It is sufficient to observe here that with the widespread growth of large, complex data processing systems and their integration into the mainstream of corporate activity, it simply will not be acceptable to have systems that are as error-ridden as are those being purveyed today. This applies whether the "purveyor" is a supplier in the public marketplace or an internal corporate department. We present some data on total system reliability in Table B.4 of Appendix B. Improvement of several orders of magnitude in the robustness of systems is becoming imperative.

To illustrate and emphasize the impact of this observation, some quantification is in order. Some spot surveys [Reynolds and Van Kinsbergen 1975] indicate that, today, well-run large data processing shops that have shunned the dubious benefits of extensive modification of their system control programs can expect a system crash about once every twelve hours; the reasons for these failures are roughly equally divided between hardware and software. An acceptable target, and one we believe is realizable, is one failure per year.

It must be understood that the kind of failure referred to here is *system* failure, not component failure. One of the most significant recent trends is the recognition that zero-defects components are not realizable, at least at commercially acceptable costs, and that systems can and should be designed to compensate for this fact. While this principle has long been understood (and occasionally employed) in hardware, it is only just now beginning to be applied to software. This trend needs to be encouraged and extended.

A problem arising from the achievement of a very low system-failure rate is that of repair when a failure does occur. Infrequent failures imply not only intolerance of failures on the part of the user, but also a lack of immediately available repair capacity when failures occur; vendors will not keep maintenance personnel on site continuously to repair once-a-year system failures. Remote diagnosis and replaceable modules contribute to a solution, but the whole question needs serious attention, because components and devices will continue to fail, even if they fail less frequently, and will therefore require repair. Increase in the mean time to failure cannot be bought at the expense of an inordinate increase in the mean time to recover.

All vendors, including many data processing departments within user companies, need to develop a great deal more sensitivity to, and understanding of, the real requirements of their customers. There remains among vendors far too much of the "We know best" attitude, which is particularly objectionable when it is not backed up by performance. This attitude is nearly absent now at senior levels, but remains a problem at lower levels, particularly among recent computer science graduates. Its most serious manifestation is the resulting failure on the part of the vendors' development and sales staffs to recognize, understand, and appreciate the reasons for user resistance to change. As a consequence, vendors fail to adequately and appropriately justify and explain needed change and to provide suitable assistance to the users to ease introduction of new concepts and tools.

6.4. Research Resources

A key parameter affecting the likelihood of finding solutions to any and all of the technological problems identified in this study is the availability of research resources, as measured by funding availability and availability of appropriately trained personnel. This is a difficult parameter to define precisely (as well as being hard to measure, whatever the definition). Furthermore, it is, to a large degree, a man-made resource and therefore seriously subject to political whim. Also, the two components, money and personnel, are subject to radically different constraints; money for research and development can appear and disappear in a period of one fiscal year, but it takes at least eight to ten years to substantially increase the available cadre of trained personnel.

In Tables B.7 and B.9 of Appendix B, we present figures on funds available for data processing research and development, and on the available data processing research and development personnel, respectively. These figures indicate, in the United States, a current expenditure of 1.27 billion dollars annually and a current personnel level of 35,400. These are substantial resources, if used rationally.

As a final thought on research and development, considering the difficulties the data processing industry finds in transferring technology from the laboratory to the field, perhaps there is too great an emphasis on maximizing the speed with which technology is transferred. Serious consideration should be given to slowing down the rate of change, thereby freeing resources for more thorough research and exploration of alternatives.

6.5. Standards

Finally, the question of the need for industrial standards in several areas of data processing is already becoming significant. The relationship of standardization to government needs, as well as the expectation of regulation, have already been discussed. There are also reasons, internal to the industry itself, prompting development and adherence to standards. A rough rule of thumb suggests, for systems of considerable complexity, a 20% additional cost due to the absence of standards, primarily as a result of the inability to buy and plug together compatible components. As noted above in Section 2 of this chapter, the most important need is for *systems* of standards that will permit complex systems to be constructed from such components. If great care is not exercised, individually useful but mutually incompatible standards may evolve. (A current example is the recent discovery that the current COBOL standard [ANSI 1974] and the draft proposal for a tape label standard are incompatible.)

7. CONCLUSIONS

We expect that the growth of the world economy will generate enormous demands for data processing systems and services. These systems and services will be essential to the management and operation of that economy. By its very nature, this expected economic growth will be critically dependent upon the development of effective and adequate data processing tools and techniques, to the point where it will force this development to occur almost without regard to cost. In order to maintain orderly economic and technical development of the data processing industry, a number of conditions, including management awareness, substantially improved total data processing system quality and reliability, increased cooperation between the industry and the higher-education system, and a sound program of standards development will be imperative. Subsequent chapters of this study examine these issues in more depth.

REFERENCES

AAU. 1973. Tax reform and crisis of financing in higher education. Washington, DC: Association of American Universities.

ABA. 1971. Monetary and Payments System Planning Committee: Executive report. Washington, DC: American Bankers Association.

ANSI. 1973. Master plan. Document X3/SD-2. New York: American National Standards Institute.

ANSI. 1974. *ANS X3.23-1974: Programming language COBOL.* New York: American National Standards Institute.

Bell, D. 1973. *The coming of post-industrial society.* New York: Basic Books.

Bloor, J. 1974. Data bank control begins in Sweden. *New Scientist* **63**:718-20.

COSATI. 1973. Report of the Committee on Scientific and Technical Information of the Federal Council on Science and Technology: Legal aspects of computerized information systems. *Honeywell Computer Journal* 7(1):Special issue.

Dantzig, G. B., and Saaty, T. L. 1973. *The compact city: A plan for a liveable urban environment.* San Francisco: W. H. Freeman.

de Grazia, S. 1964. *Of time, work, and leisure.* Garden City, NY: Doubleday.

de Jouvenel, B. 1967. *The art of conjecture.* New York: Basic Books.

Dickson, P. 1971. *Think tanks.* New York: Atheneum.

Dunn, E. S., Jr. 1971. *Economics and social development.* Baltimore, MD: Johns Hopkins Univ. Press.

Feistel, H. 1973. Cryptography and computer privacy. *Scientific American* **228**(5):15-23.

Forrester, J. W. 1971. *World dynamics.* Cambridge, MA: Wright-Allen Press.

JCUDI. 1972. The plan for information society: A national goal toward year 2000. Computerization Committee Final Report. 3-2-5 Kasumigaseki, Chiyodaku, Tokyo: Japan Computer Usage Development Institute.

Kahn, D. 1967. *The codebreakers: The story of secret writing.* New York: Macmillan.

Kahn, H. 1970. *The emerging Japanese superstate: Challenge and response.* New York: Prentice-Hall.

———, and Bruce-Briggs, B. 1972. *Things to come: Thinking about the seventies and eighties.* New York: Macmillan.

———, and Wiener, A. J. 1967. *The year 2000: A framework for speculation on the next thirty-three years.* New York: Macmillan.

Linstone, H. A. 1974. Planning: Toy or tool? *IEEE Spectrum* **11**(4):42-49.

Meadows, D. H., Meadows, D. L., Rangers, J., and Behrens, W. W. 1972. *The limits to growth. A report for the Club of Rome's project on the predicament of mankind.* New York: Universe Books.

Nolan, R. L. 1973. Computer data bases: The future is now. *Harvard Business Review* **51**(5):98-114.

Perlmutter, H. V. 1971. The multinational corporation: A new kind of institution. Diebold Professional Paper No. 38. New York: Diebold Group Research Program.

Pollack, G. A. 1974. The economic consequences of the energy crisis. *Foreign Affairs* **52**(3):452-71.

Reynolds, C. H., and Van Kinsbergen, J. E. 1975. Tracking reliability and availability. *Datamation* **21**(11):106-16.

Robertson, W. 1973. Those daring young con men of Equity Funding. *Fortune* **88**(2):81-85,120-32 (August).

Rostovtzeff, M. 1927. *A history of the ancient world,* vol. II: *Rome.* London: Oxford Univ. Press.

Senders, J. W. 1963. Information storage requirements for the contents of the world's libraries. *Science* **141**:1067-68.

Singer, C., Holmyard, E. J., Hall, A. R., and Williams, T. I. 1956. *A history of technology,* vol. II. London: Oxford Univ. Press.

Starr, C., and Rudman, R. 1973. Parameters of technological growth. *Science* **182**:358-64.

Steel, T. B., Jr. 1974. Data base systems: Implications for commerce and industry. In *Data base management systems (Proc. 1973 SHARE Working Conference on Data Base Management Systems),* ed. D. A. Jardine, pp. 219-34. New York: American Elsevier.

Toffler, A. 1970. *Future shock.* New York: Random House.

Westin, A. F., and Baker, M. A. 1972. *Data banks in a free society.* New York: Quadrangle.

Wylie, K. 1971. Summary of results: GUIDE/IBM study of advanced applications. 111 E. Wacker Dr., Chicago, IL 60601: GUIDE International.

3

USERS

The material object[s] . . . *can't be right
or wrong. . . . They don't have any ethical
codes to follow except those people give
them. The test of the machine is the
satisfaction it gives you. There isn't any
other test. If the machine produces
tranquillity it's right. If it disturbs you
it's wrong until either the machine or your
mind is changed.*

R. M. Pirsig

1. INTRODUCTION

The growth projections of the data processing industry and the
economic projections of Chapter 2 depend upon the success that the
data processing industry will achieve in satisfying the needs of the
users—the people who want or require a data processing system to perform some task on their behalf. These users are the only reason for
the existence of data processing systems. We shall first attempt to
describe the characteristics and the expectations of these users.

By 1985, almost all segments of society will include individuals who
can be thought of as users of data processing systems—individuals who
are affected by, or are dependent upon data processing in their daily
work. Boehm [1973] estimates that, by 1985, over 70% of the U.S.
labor force will be so dependent. These users' requirements will vary
greatly, depending on their jobs and on how they interact with the data
processing system. The following (arbitrarily ordered) lists suggest the
range of user needs, roles, and methods of operation, and provide some
insight into the capabilities that data processing systems must provide
to fulfill user expectations.

1.1. User Characteristics

Users of data processing facilities, their needs, and their *modi operandi* can be described by means of a number of characteristics:

- batch vs. interactive (or, more accurately, real-time, interactive, and batch, the last with and without deadline scheduling);
- novice vs. experienced;
- programmer vs. user of "canned" packages[1] (the numerical balance will shift, with time, to the canned-package user);
- occasional vs. full-time;
- small (who needs a little more than a desk calculator) vs. large (weather prediction);
- numeric (orbital calculations, econometric models) vs. nonnumeric (update of a data base, text processing, pattern recognition);
- high-level language (FORTRAN, COBOL, PL/I) vs. low-level language (assembler, e.g., in input/output error-recovery routines);
- central-processor limited ("number crunching") vs. input/output limited (sorting of large files);
- "solo" vs. local team vs. geographically dispersed team;
- unscheduled (one-time research computation, one-time management report) vs. scheduled or periodic (payroll, plant scheduling);
- routine (data entry or credit-card validation) vs. state-of-the-art (image processing);
- isolated, time-sharing terminal user who may, at best, know the procedure for logging onto a system vs. the user surrounded by data processing experts;
- standard default user vs. one who wants to use the system in novel and unexpected ways;
- multiprocessed vs. single-thread user (some users will want to initiate the processing of more than one task at a time).

These characteristics are not, by any means, independent of one another, but many of them are nearly so.

1.2. User Expectations

It is axiomatic in the data processing industry that users who admit to being completely satisfied with the data processing facilities available to them lose face by such an admission. But even after we discount the effects of this tradition, there remain the two following facts:

---

1. There is a problem of definition of terms here: is a user of, say, IMS [IBM 1973] a programmer or a user of a canned package?

- users' needs are not adequately fulfilled today; and
- users' needs and expectations increase and expand with time.

The remainder of this study is concerned with means for adequately fulfilling users' needs. As for expectations, we observe that the Parkinson-like effect of rising expectations is, in fact, a well-justified, well-documented, and continuing phenomenon. As an example, in the batch world of the 1950's, one hour's downtime was accepted as a matter of course; today, such a downtime causes some discomfort; ten years hence, in the on-line environment of the 1980's, it will have very deleterious effects.

The following is a list of some of the qualitative expectations that users have today, or shortly will have:

- *Reliability and availability* (of the *entire* data processing facility, with communications links, terminals, data bases, etc.: all of the facilities that affect service to the end user) approaching that of the No. 1 ESS telephone central office [Clement, Jones, and Watters 1974]. This implies, among others, the following capabilities (which should be automatic and invisible to the end user):
  - fail-soft (the failure of one component should not cause the failure of the entire system);
  - checkpoint, backup, restart;
  - on-line maintenance, diagnostics, repairs;
  - dynamic reconfiguration;
  - automatic retry;
  - etc.

- *Consistency* of the entire user interface. The data processing facility must present a single, uniform interface to a user, and, furthermore, that interface must *always* interact with the user in that user's "source" language. This is the "single active agent" concept [Baker 1967]. Thus, users will expect, among other things:
  - uniform (and comprehensible) error messages, warnings, prompts, etc.;
  - uniform command language, editor, "debuggers," etc.;
  - uniform behavior in case of errors, "abends," etc. (e.g., *all* of the output must be delivered to the user, as opposed to having varying amounts of it hidden or lost within the system);
  - uniform and consistent defaults;
  - uniform number conversion and computational algorithms;
  - etc.

- *Understandability* of the externals of the system. This implies, in addition to some of the above:
  - user-oriented, easily understood documentation;
  - ability to describe the system's external behavior without recourse to a description of the system's internals;
  - existence of well-defined boundaries for the applicability of various rules, constructs, etc., that can be discovered without extensive experimentation [Baker 1967];
  - liberal application of the principle of "minimum astonishment";
  - etc.

- *Simplicity, smoothness,* and *naturalness* in:
  - protocols (logging on, file sharing, etc.);
  - protection (which should be available, but which users must not be saddled with whether they need it or not);
  - defaults;
  - documentation and other such aids;
  - command languages;
  - etc.

- *Control* (where required) over the flow of processing and over the resources and procedures used during that process.

- *Friendliness, forgiveness,* and *robustness,* so that one user's error has *no* effect on the system or on other users, and as non-catastrophic an effect on the erring user as possible. By this we mean that, if possible, an error should be reported to the user *before* it causes a catastrophe, rather than after. Furthermore, the user's error should be clearly indicated to him. We must remember that nothing alienates users more than not getting results through no (apparent) fault of their own. We will return briefly to the topic of robustness, but from a somewhat different point of view, in Section 4.6 of Chapter 6.

Finally, users must be able to "multiprocess" themselves, so that they can do productive work (e.g., prepare input at terminals) when other tasks of theirs are being processed.

1.3. A Taxonomy of the User Population

In order to determine the requirements for future data processing systems, we have organized our discussion of user needs around three subgroups within the broad population of users: *end users, mid users,* and *system support users.*

The end users are the data processing system's real beneficiaries. They use the system's output or results to perform their jobs or other activities. They are not necessarily acquainted with data processing technology and, in fact, usually care little about the details of data processing systems. To them, data processing is simply one service among many they might employ to solve their problems or to perform their tasks. Whether they employ it is dependent on how easy it is to use and on its accuracy, timeliness, and cost.

The mid users are those who interpret the end users' needs and develop the procedures a data processing system applies to obtain solutions to the problems posed by the end users. The mid users desire a data processing facility that is readily available, that allows them to express the problem in terms that are natural to the problem being solved, and that provides feedback and responses in terms that are understandable to them and to the end users. These criteria imply a stable, reliable environment in which the mid users can describe the processing procedures to be followed in such a way that they need not be concerned with the internal details of the data processing system, the specific resources used, the particular methods used to access data files and to communicate with remote terminals, the internal language of the system, etc.

The system support users are the data processing system's custodians, responsible for the system's maintenance and well-being. This group provides the basic data processing environment and the mid users' interface to it. Each member of the system support group is a data processing systems expert who should be concerned with the optimization of resource utilization, the development of scheduling procedures to satisfy the end and mid users, the physical custody of the installation's data bases, the installation of the required system security methods, etc. One of the main responsibilities of system support users is the maintenance and improvement of the Installation Control Program—ICP—that governs the system's operation (see Section 4 below). The major concerns of this class of users are system reliability and security, accessibility of the functions provided by the system, and diagnostic and monitoring capabilities. These users must have facilities with which to dynamically observe, modify, and correct the installation's system components (as contrasted with the vendor-supplied System Control Program—SCP—which they should consider inviolate), but without interfering with the work of any other user of the system.

The activities of each of these user groups must be supported satis-factorily for the system to be a success; failure to support any one group will result in a breakdown of the total system. The system will not be responsive to the end user's needs if the mid user fails to develop a usable procedure. The mid users will be unable to complete their tasks in a timely manner if the system is difficult to communicate with. A vendor's failure to provide a stable base with all of the func-tions required by the system support users will thwart them in their job. In the remainder of this chapter, we identify the problems that must be solved if the needs of all these users are to be met.

2. THE END USER

The end user population can be divided into three subgroups, which we label *indirect, intermediate,* and *direct,* respectively. The largest sub-group, that of *indirect* end users, includes all of the people who are sup-ported by data processing systems in their daily activities, even though, for the most part, they do not deal directly with these systems. They are the executives who request reports from members of their staffs, customers who buy on credit, airline passengers who make reserva-tions, etc. As a rule, they have no interest in how the system works as long as their needs are met: that is, as long as the data processing system provides the services they desire at what they consider to be reasonable costs. A failure to provide these services is a failure of the entire data processing system in these users' eyes, and they will judge that system accordingly.

Data processing systems exist mainly to serve this group; without these users, there is little point in there being a system. There is no easy way to generalize the needs of this group; in fact, most of its members would have difficulty in stating their individual data pro-cessing needs. But they will have no trouble determining when service falls below their expectations: a bill's arrival after it is due, overbooking of a flight, erroneous or delayed deliveries of goods, etc. Extreme care must therefore be taken to build into the system sufficient safeguards to guard against these types of errors. Murphy's Law[2] must be remem-bered at all times, and vigilance is required to minimize the number of such failures and errors.

---

2. "If anything can go wrong, it surely will."

The members of the second subgroup of end users, the *intermediate* end users, specify the problems the data processing system is to solve. This group of users may also possess little or no technical knowledge about data processing per se; their expertise is in the functional areas to which data processing can provide assistance: marketing, manufacturing, accounting, education, etc. They are responsible for identifying, with help from other disciplines (including data processing), the activities in their respective areas that can benefit from the use of a data processing system, and for working with the mid users to develop solutions to the problems identified.

Historically, the intermediate end user has had great difficulty in stating his needs in a manner understandable by those who were responsible for their implementation. Not only has there been difficulty in developing precise definitions of the problems, but there has not been any formal way, except in some narrow technical areas, of communicating these definitions to the implementors. If the efficiency of the development process is to be substantially improved, both of these areas must be attacked. An example of end user and mid user communication engendered with the help of an interactive applications generator is proposed in Section 5.7 of Chapter 6. Procedures that help end users determine all situations that might occur during the execution of their applications system must be developed, as must the means for end users to describe (in a rigorous form that can be readily understood by mid users and, ultimately, by the system itself) the actions to be taken in these situations. Failure to develop these facilities will seriously hamper the growth of data processing applications.

The third group of end users are the *direct* end users. There are two types of direct end users. The first consists of the clerks, technicians, accountants, and operational personnel who routinely use the system to perform their daily tasks. We expect that, by 1985, much of the input data will be collected automatically (by sensors, etc.). However, a large amount of data will still be collected manually—primarily through direct interaction with the system, but, in many cases, without the end user being aware of it. That is, whatever information is required by the system will be acquired as an automatic by-product of the user's normal activities of taking an order, recording a sale, performing a credit check, taking damaged inventory out of stock, etc. We believe that there will be a significant reduction in the need for dedicated data-input clerks to translate such data into machine-readable form.

Direct end users of the second type have most of the attributes of indirect, intermediate, and direct users, as well as some of the attributes of mid users. They conceive the problem, formulate the solution, and use the system to obtain the solution: they are the "classical" time-sharing users. Many of the home terminal users described in Section 5 of Chapter 4 will also fall into this category. Their usage is highly unstructured and cannot be preplanned. This imposes many additional requirements on the system, such as the system's ability to guide these users through areas with which they are unfamiliar, while safeguarding the rest of the system's users. There will not be any significant reduction of the end user's dependence upon the mid user until the system is able to handle this function well.

While there are already many direct end users, systems that *truly* accommodate their needs have not yet been built. Most of today's systems are unreliable, slow, and unnatural and difficult to use. All of these shortcomings can, we believe, be substantially overcome by 1985 with a properly disciplined approach to system design in the following areas:

- *A natural, easy to use, consistent interface to the data processing system* (as "transparent" as possible), so that the user is not forced to interact with the system in an awkward and unnatural manner. This implies the ability to communicate with the system through the spoken or written word, pictures, finger pointing, and other procedures that are natural to the individual. It also implies the development and cataloging of vocabularies and grammars specific to individual disciplines.

- *Systems designed to minimize human errors.* This means simple, stable procedures involving little more than manual dexterity—and, therefore, relatively little training—that can for the most part be directed by the system itself. If an error occurs, the correction procedures must be carefully designed for each possible situation, and under no circumstance must the user be left to recover as best he can. Rather, the system must be able to assist and, if necessary, guide the user through the appropriate remedial steps.

- *Response timing consistent with the user's requirements and expectations.* System response times should be geared to the user's most effective work speed, as judged by the intermediate end user. Where a response is required to serve a customer who is on the telephone, that response should be essentially immediate. Where lengthy calculations or data searches are required, a longer time can be tolerated. However, it is very important to minimize the system's response time to the on-line user in order to avoid the deterioration of user efficiency that occurs when the system's response time becomes unduly long [Doherty, Thompson, and Boies 1972].

- *Reliability and availability.* If the data processing system is to be used in the way a desk calculator is used by an accountant or a hand-held calculator is used by an engineer, then it must be as reliable and available as these tools. This means a significant improvement in system availability and reliability over what is experienced today.

Successful growth of data processing depends upon the development of solutions to these problems. If solutions are not obtained, end users will either continue to do things in the same old way, or seek alternative methods that, in their opinion, provide them with better control and better fulfill their expectations.

3. THE MID USER

In today's terminology, the mid user can best be thought of as a combination of programmer, analyst, and methods person. His job is to design and construct applications systems within the data processing environment provided by the system support user, to be used by the direct end user in obtaining the solution to the problems posed by the intermediate end user. The mid user is responsible for developing complete applications systems that optimize the productivity of all the people and equipment involved, while holding development and maintenance costs to a minimum.

That the mid user will need to exist at all in 1985 is, in a way, unfortunate. If the design and maintenance of data processing systems did not demand the high level of understanding of data processing details that it does (and that it will, in all likelihood, continue to do), then the end user could construct the required systems directly, and the inefficiencies of communicating the problem from the end user to the mid user and, finally, to the system could be eliminated.

In determining how best to improve the productivity of the mid user, it is worth examining the following six task areas which consume the mid user's time.

3.1. Understanding of End User Requirements

The first and foremost problem for the mid user is to fully understand the end user's requirements and expectations, and, when a solution has been obtained, to determine whether it fits the original requirements. The end user must describe and the mid user must understand, as completely as possible:

- the application itself;
- the input data;
- the required outputs;
- the expected workload.

This problem is discussed in Section 2 above and touched upon in Section 5.1 of Chapter 6. However, it should be pointed out that, as the requirements become more and more complicated, generating adequate solutions will require more detailed and more intense dialogs between the end user and the mid user during the design and implementation phase in order to adequately evaluate all of the available trade-offs and alternatives.

3.2. System Design

The design of the applications system is the most critical and often the most time-consuming of the mid user's tasks, because the design dictates the amount of effort that will be required to implement the system, as well as the system's ultimate operational efficiency. It would appear that it will still be necessary to design systems in a step-by-step fashion in 1985. This process will continue to be complicated by the need for the mid user to:

- know many details of data processing technology, which, in all likelihood, will continue to be as complex as it is today;
- be knowledgeable in the end users' area of expertise;
- know the direct end users' capabilities and limitations, so that applications systems do not place unrealistic demands on such users;
- be a skillfull practitioner in a craft that has no underlying scientific basis;
- provide for ways to accommodate changes in needs, capabilities, and technology.

Refinements of top-down design and chief programmer techniques will provide some help in this area, but these techniques will not reduce the requirement for technological sophistication that makes this one of the more difficult functions to transfer to the end user.

3.3. Implementation

More energy is being spent in trying to improve the mid user's efficiency in the area of implementation than in any other. New languages, data-base and resource-management procedures, structured programming techniques, etc., have all helped to ease the load, but the mid user still has to be a specialist in order to translate a problem statement into a working applications system. More natural languages (including the command interface) must be developed to allow the mid users (and, eventually, the end users) to state the developed solutions in terms that are meaningful within their respective areas of expertise, without requiring them to learn the idiosyncrasies of the data processing system.

Of equal importance is the development of a specialized "language" for teaching end users how to use a system. Today, English is the only available instructional medium. It is unsatisfactory because it lacks precision and is highly prone to ambiguity. A better medium should be found.

3.4. Testing

No one has yet been able to determine, either through testing or through more formalized proofs, whether a program is entirely accurate, even if the question of whether it solves the problem that was originally posed is disregarded. A means for ensuring, with a much higher degree of certainty than is possible today, that the final system will not fail must continue to be sought.

No discussion of testing can overlook the necessity of devising ways to test a new system without disrupting the current system. Many errors that occur at the time of system changeover, or soon thereafter, are due primarily to inadequate testing. It is rarely possible to create an artificial test environment that duplicates the real environment. The possibility of running two systems—the current and the test systems simultaneously, with the results compared automatically—should be explored as a means of achieving more thorough testing. This problem is particularly difficult, and particularly important, with on-line systems.

3.5. Installation

Solving the aforementioned problems will go a long way toward providing a solution to the problem of installing new applications systems (or new versions of existing systems). Beyond that, if means are developed for documenting the system and preparing instructions for the user, it should then be possible to successfully teach the user how to best use the system. Failure to produce documentation for the user and to teach the user how to use the system have been major stumbling blocks to successful installation of applications systems.

3.6. Maintenance

It is estimated that, on the average, more than twice the original development cost is spent in maintaining a system during its lifetime. Maintenance activity results from any one of three circumstances:

- changes in the user environment or requirements (planned or not);
- errors in the original system;
- changes in the data processing system.

Solutions to the problems outlined in the first five of the mid user's task areas will help to reduce the number of occurrences of the first two of these cases, as well as to reduce the cost and time needed to resolve each such occurrence. However, vendors must also provide applications interfaces that remain consistent and stable despite any system changes that the vendors may introduce.

Providing solutions to the problems outlined above will improve the productivity of the mid user. As these solutions appear, they will allow the mid user to shift his attention away from the details of the data processing system and toward the applications design and development tasks involved in meeting end users' requirements.

4. THE SYSTEM SUPPORT USER AND THE ICP CONCEPT

The system support user group is made up of the installation's data processing systems experts. They are responsible for creating and maintaining the installation's data processing facility through the interfaces they build to the vendor-supplied hardware and system control software. It is their job to consult with the mid users, helping them select the proper programming languages and system functions to optimize their applications systems. Therefore, they will continue to require a knowledge of the mid users' requirements. The system support users are the custodians of the installation's data and systems files, and they are the group responsible for providing the means to attain and maintain data processing security.

The system support users determine the installation's operating efficiency through the environment they provide and the operating procedures they install. To optimize the system, they need a great deal of detailed information about the applications to be run on the system and about the system's performance. This information is required both dynamically, in order to maximize throughput and to help spot developing bottlenecks, and on a summary basis, in order to tune the system and to build simulations for evaluating future requirements and improvements. Performance guidelines for each system unit and application program should serve as threshold values that cause alarms to be given whenever performance falls below these values, thus alerting the system support group to potential system weaknesses.

The system support group should control the use of the system by means of an Installation Control Program (ICP) that serves as the interface to the vendor-supplied System Control Program (SCP). This ICP will, for the most part, be made up of modules (or "primitives") supplied by the vendor, thus giving the system support group the capability, through the ICP, of controlling and monitoring the system's functions and resources in order to optimize their use in the installation's environment. The ICP (unlike the SCP) is *not* inviolate; system support users will be able to, and will, modify it so that it meets the needs of the installation. To allow this, the ICP will contain all the functions an installation must be able to modify. ICP modules will be capable of being changed, and even replaced, by the system support users [Dolotta and Irvine 1969]. The structure of the ICP must minimize the system support users' chances of interfering with or changing the calculation processes of the other users of the system. Because current systems do not provide this protection, long hours of work at inconvenient times are required of the system support users, and even then there is no way to test each new system modification adequately enough to ensure that it works. Just as with mid users' new programs, it will be necessary to develop methods for dynamically testing new system features, comparing new and previous test results, displaying any discrepancies, and "backing out" any incorrect results. Although this is likely to be very costly, no other procedure appears capable of providing the required continuity of operations while still allowing dynamic system modifications and improvements.

The ICP provides the interface between the system and the application programs. The ICP must be designed to make the mid users less concerned with the internals of the system and free them from the effects of the various modifications, improvements, and other perturbations of the system that result from the activities of the system support users. Even when changes are made to provide additional functions, they must not invalidate existing programs and user knowledge: what works today must work tomorrow. It is reasonable to expect that the mid user will expend some effort to stay abreast of the evolving data processing system environment. This effort will of necessity be small and will consequently mandate long periods before an "obsolete" function is allowed to disappear from the system.

The system support user, in his role of data custodian who is implementing the policies of the data-base administrator, is responsible for determining the media to be used for data storage, the organization of the data on these media, the methods of access to the data, and the means for protecting the data. It is up to the system support user to see that the data required by a job are provided in a timely manner, as well as to optimize the combination of data-storage usage and data-access time over the entire spectrum of jobs the system must perform. This implies the need to collect considerable amounts of detailed information about the usage of data by the various jobs and about the effects of such usage on the system and on user tasks. This information is required in order to determine the proper access procedures, storage and migration strategies, security and protection schemes, resource requirements, and backup and reconstruction needs. When the results call for modification of storage-management methods, means must be provided to do this dynamically (and invisibly to the mid and end users) while the system continues to operate.

While security of data is the most obvious security need in a data processing installation, the system support user must be aware of other potential threats and their legal implications:

- unauthorized system resource usage;
- destruction or modification of the system itself;
- theft;
- capturing (or interfering with) data transmission;
- natural disasters (fires, floods, etc.);
- insurrection, sabotage, war, malicious mischief, etc.;
- violation of privacy safeguards.

Means for safeguarding against all of these must be available to the system support user and to the installation management to use as necessary.

5. CONCLUSIONS

The data processing system must be able to adequately serve *all* of its users. It must provide the functions and capabilities the users expect, in a manner the users expect, when needed, and at a cost the users consider reasonable. Users must be made to feel more comfortable with the system, and be made confident that they will obtain, in a timely manner, the results they require. The problems involved in providing such an environment in the areas of applications systems, hardware, software, and management are the subjects of the following chapters of this study.

REFERENCES

Baker, C. L. 1967. JOSS: Rubrics. Report P-3560. Santa Monica, CA 90406: Rand Corp.

Boehm, B. W. 1973. Software and its impact: A quantitative assessment. *Datamation* **19**(5):48-59.

Clement, G. F., Jones, W. C., and Watters, R. J. 1974. No. 1 ESS processors: How dependable have they been? *Bell Laboratories Record* **52**(1):21-25.

Doherty, W. J., Thompson, C. H., and Boies, S. J. 1972. An analysis of interactive system usage with respect to software, linguistic, and scheduling attributes. *Proc. IEEE International Conference on Cybernetics and Society,* pp. 113-19. New York: Institute of Electrical and Electronics Engineers.

Dolotta, T. A., and Irvine, C. A. 1969. Proposal for a time sharing command structure. *Information Processing 68 (Proc. IFIP Congress 1968),* vol. 1, pp. 493-98. Amsterdam: North-Holland.

IBM. 1973. Information Management System/360—Version 2: General information manual. Form GH20-0765. 1501 California Ave., Palo Alto, CA 94303: IBM Corp.

4

APPLICATIONS

*It is well to remember that in assembling
our machines . . . all parts should go
together without being forced. If—for any
reason—you are unable to assemble any
of the parts, you should examine them
thoroughly to locate the trouble. . . . If
you cannot get them together, there must
be a reason. By all means, do not use
a hammer.*

Repair manual for the IBM
computing meat scale

1. INTRODUCTION

In this chapter, we predict some general characteristics of the data processing applications that are likely to exist within the corporate business environment during the 1980-1985 period, and we discuss some
possible uses of computers in the home. Chapter 6 will discuss the
software tools and techniques required to develop these applications.
We focus on the business environment because that is where the
major use of data processing has taken place since the middle 1950's,
and we believe that this will continue to be the case in the future.
Moreover, we believe that business applications exhibit many characteristics that will also apply to data processing applications in government, military (primarily command-and-control), and educational (e.g.,
computer-aided and computer-managed instruction) environments. All
of these applications appear to share similar basic requirements for on-
line teleprocessing, real-time operation, large data bases, security,
reliability, and availability.

2. BACKGROUND AND THE PAST

It may be helpful to characterize, in a general way, some of the functions of a business enterprise, in order to describe the changing characteristics of business data processing applications. In the abstract, an
enterprise can be represented by a set of concentric circles. The inner-
most circle represents the top management function. Further out are
the (usually centralized) financial and accounting functions. Still
further out are the operational functions: manufacturing, distribution,
warehousing, etc. The outermost layer represents the marketing functions and customer services with their external (customer and consumer) interfaces. This description is not intended to be a particularly
meaningful way to view a business enterprise as such; rather, it is
intended to provide a framework for discussing the characteristics of
business data processing applications.

Business data processing applications of the 1950's and of the early
1960's were almost exclusively devoted to automation of accounting
and financial activities, with only minimal concern for and assistance to
top management (inward functions), or the operations, marketing, and
consumer services (outward functions). The traditional batch business
applications, such as accounts payable, accounts receivable, payroll, and
general ledger, are examples of this early trend. In the early 1970's, an
increasing number of companies appear to have mastered this class of
batch accounting and financial applications, and it seems that almost all
such applications in these companies have been implemented and are
operational. These applications provide little or no *new* information to
top management for planning and control, and little or no new information for operational management. An increasing emphasis is beginning to be placed on systems that provide information to operational
management and that help it in the exercise of control. Although this
is something of an oversimplification, it is essentially true that the
number of *new batch* business applications being implemented (as a
fraction of all new applications) is declining at present in many
companies.

In the late 1950's and in the 1960's, an *independent* set of applications in the operations research area was beginning to serve operational
management and, to a very limited extent, top management. During
the same period, the U.S. armed services were grappling with the problem of providing their top and operational managements with secure
and reliable real-time command-and-control systems.

There continues to be a need to provide top management with information that is useful for control and planning purposes. There have been many attempts at fulfilling this need. Very few efforts to support top-management functions by means of data processing applications have been successful, especially attempts to support top management's planning activities. A variety of operations research applications, (e.g., scheduling and optimization of manufacturing activities, distribution scheduling, and inventory control) have been developed for operational management. These applications often were among the most profitable ones for the enterprise; however, their major drawback is that they are case-study oriented, utilizing either historical or projected data. They allow very substantial savings and increase opportunities, but they are primarily oriented to producing "guideline" operational plans. Although highly profitable on that basis, they do not provide the means for the enterprise to react in a realistic and timely fashion to changes in the business environment, and therefore they are not capable of realizing the great profit potential inherent in the ability to so react.

Another type of data processing applications, often referred to as "scientific and engineering" applications, began to appear in the early and middle 1950's. (These applications are somewhat different from business applications in that, in general, they tend *not* to make direct use of corporate business data.) They have, since that time, continued to expand into a large number of different areas. There have been, with some minor exceptions, two basic modes of operation in using these applications:

- The use of "canned" (packaged) programs, which are used repeatedly by different users to solve different problems of the same general type.

- The use of user-generated applications, which the end users have "developed" (i.e., specified or programmed) to solve a unique problem, or to study a "non-standard" solution to a fairly standard problem.

The major characteristics of these applications have been their expansion rate and the installation of terminals (time-sharing, etc.) that allow end users to access remotely located data processing systems from their own locations. Some interactive applications have been developed, but the vast majority are still remote-access batch applications, as opposed to truly interactive applications.

3. THE FUTURE

In the future, the main thrusts in business applications development efforts will be to:

• provide timely data to operational management and, to a minor extent, to top management;

• apply operations research techniques to actual operating data on a timely (and sometimes real-time) basis, in order to provide dynamic optimization, scheduling, and guideline information to the operations personnel;

• realize the full profit potential of data processing applications within the functions of operational management, marketing, and customer services.

In essence, the data processing applications of the future will move out from the centralized business functions into the operations area and further out to the interface between marketing and customers. This is a significant change in applications characteristics and requirements. The American Airlines' SABRE system [Plugge and Perry 1961] was an early example of an application at the marketing and customer interface. The current banking and point-of-sale systems indicate the accelerating trend in this direction. Such systems provide services at the customer interface, to operational management, and to centralized business functions. This type of system will be seen in many businesses in the 1980-1985 time period.

There will be a definite attempt to implement a different set of applications to aid top management in planning and control activities. The data processing industry is rapidly developing the capabilities necessary to produce systems for planning and control required by the various levels of operational management. To date, however, there have been very few successful attempts to provide planning systems for top management. It appears that the type of planning done at top-management levels requires qualitatively different types of systems than are required for planning at operational levels, especially with regard to a high tolerance for ambiguity. The activities of top management may be thought of as designing and implementing procedures and policies under which the operational activities of the enterprise can work. Data processing is not (at present) a tool for developing such designs, but it might be thought of as affording additional design options for possible implementation. In any event, the data processing industry still has a great deal to learn about the requirements for systems meant to be used in support of top management. Such systems will have to be adaptable to many different styles of management and planning.

The growth in the use of terminals for rapid, decentralized access will continue, and scientific applications will continue to expand into new areas.

A very promising expansion area for data processing applications is the automation of many, if not most, office functions, namely data entry, distribution, and retrieval, as well as text processing, document preparation, communications, etc. We believe that, over the next ten years, the potential market for applications aimed at such "offices of the future" may well equal the value of all of today's business data processing applications. The emergence of such automated offices may cause administrative readjustments in some enterprises, as we point out in Section 4.4 of Chapter 7.

The availability of interactive capabilities on in-house, general-purpose computers (as opposed to time-sharing utility networks) is causing a major expansion into the truly interactive scientific and engineering applications areas. We expect this trend to accelerate.

4. IMPLICATIONS

The uses of business data for optimizing operations, for planning, for management reports, etc., will introduce the requirement that most transaction data (which are presently captured only for accounting purposes) be captured at or near their source in real (or nearly real) time for use in operational control systems and for subsequent use as accounting data. This requirement will also stimulate the introduction of data processing systems into marketing and other consumer-oriented applications areas, and it will allow dynamic operations research applications to become a reality. The services provided by these applications will cause a rapid increase in the number of individuals who benefit from data processing, as well as in the number of individuals who actually use data processing in the performance of their functions [Boehm 1973].

Businesses, recognizing that most of their work forces perform tasks that are governed by set procedures, will progress toward embedding these procedures within data processing applications. Existing operational applications will be increasingly interconnected, in some cases resulting in highly integrated data processing systems. The overall result will be that business data processing will progress far beyond simple extensions of today's applications, and some enterprises will make significant progress toward "total enterprise systematization." Applications leading toward a "cashless/checkless" society will be at least partially in place. Order-to-ship systems will track and schedule all pertinent activities and the utilization of all pertinent resources leading to shipping, solely on the basis of the entry of an order. Increasingly, then, all individuals in the enterprise will receive direct data processing support and will, by the same token, become more and more dependent on that support in the performance of their respective daily duties.

Businesses will proceed to implement sensor-based systems that will utilize data processing to react to a number of conditions that are largely ignored in today's applications. These systems will allow "automatic" modification of sensor-driven tasks in response to changes in design, materials, or specifications. Information derived from sensors will be increasingly available and used to assist in the operation of an enterprise.

Business enterprises, governmental agencies, and other common-interest groups will pool resources and implement applications that today cannot, for economic, legal, and other reasons, be implemented and maintained by a single entity. These applications will provide common solutions acceptable to all parties sharing a common problem. On-line tariff calculation systems for railroads and area-irrigation models that can be accessed by individual farmers are examples of such applications. The legal concerns raised by the phenomenon of many firms within a single industry cooperating in developing solutions that are then shared by members of an industry group will be resolved in many instances; as a result, new industry associations that provide common data processing services to all their members may come into being. Where a well-defined market exists, service entrepreneurs will develop applications aimed at broad sets of customers or individuals. Similarly, governmental agencies will develop applications that will support many groups, entities, and individuals by providing capabilities that fall within the scope of each such agency [Wylie 1971].

The expansion of applications will be significantly influenced by the increasing use and availability of remote terminals and of associated computing and communications facilities. The ability to access a data processing facility that utilizes real-time data in generating its responses to user queries will increase the value of that facility to the end user. This increased value will economically justify the various added expenses for terminals and associated communications facilities. This trend toward increased availability of terminals, remote-access facilities, etc., also encourages very small users of data processing, as well as users who have highly specialized needs that cannot be economically satisfied by their in-house facilities, to use time-sharing "utility" services.

Three clear trends emerge as key characteristics of new business applications that will be developed over the next ten years. First is the progressive integration of various applications into a coherent and continuous set that supports essentially all activities in an enterprise. This continuous set of integrated applications will require the ability to share data and to communicate decisions. This ability is beginning to appear in the advanced, sophisticated, data-base oriented systems currently beginning to be specified and designed. There will be increasing pressure to implement such *sets* of applications. Second, these applications will interface *directly* with individual users throughout the enterprise. Terminal equipment as well as the applications themselves will have to be designed to be "people-proof" and conducive to efficient and error-free use by many different kinds of users. The third trend will be the increasing use of data processing in management and in research and discovery efforts. With vast amounts of coherent data available within an enterprise as a result of integrating many, if not most, applications, there will be increasing pressure for access to and use of current information in the discovery processes. Free-form search and correlation capabilities driven by "English-like" languages will continue to be developed and expanded, but their ultimate usefulness remains to be proven.

The resulting systems will have some or all of the following characteristics:

- Real-time source data capture will cause an expansion in the use of terminals and data transmission that is best described as an explosion.

- The amount of data that will be required on line, as well as the many uses of that data, will introduce sophisticated requirements for secure, data-base oriented systems and will force a very fast growth in random-access storage hardware.

- Many of these systems will introduce a dependence on data processing for the handling of consumer transactions, as is the situation today with the various airline reservations systems. If the data processing system is unavailable, unreliable, or unresponsive, sales and revenues may be lost. These requirements for system availability, reliability, and responsiveness have in the past been both rare and very expensive to satisfy. They are rapidly becoming commonplace, and they will have to be satisfied. For some applications, such as supermarket point-of-sale systems, computer hierarchies of micro-, mini-, midi-, and maxicomputers, interconnected by communications facilities, will be used to meet reliability requirements. However, some major applications (e.g., airline reservations systems) will, by their very nature, require highly centralized data and transaction processing, and these types of applications present the most difficult reliability problems.

- The size of these applications (by any measure—e.g., cost, man-years of analysis and design) will increase significantly—by at least an order of magnitude—as compared to today's systems. Their complexity will grow even faster. This growth will be coupled with the almost absolute reliability requirement mentioned above for hardware and applications. The cumulative effect of the great increase in size, the very much increased complexity, and the extremely stringent requirements for uninterruptible and error-free operation is the prime cause of the problems that are fast coming upon the data processing industry. These trends emphasize the productivity problems and the "expectation gap" problems that plague state-of-the-art systems today.

These trends and implications are derived primarily from looking at data processing applications in a business enterprise. The GUIDE/IBM Delphi Study [Wylie 1971] and other studies indicate similar trends and implications in the area of government applications. Military command-and-control systems have long experienced the problems of complexity, interactive behavior, and very high reliability requirements discussed above. Educational institutions' plans for computer-assisted and computer-managed instruction systems suggest that they, too, will develop similar requirements. We believe, therefore, that these trends and implications are general in character and are not restricted to the business environment.

The above discussion has focused on large, integrated applications because that is where the major applications growth will occur and where the major problems that can limit such growth will appear. We cannot ignore, however, the growth that will result from mini-computers. Minicomputers will appear as intelligent terminals, as concentrators, and as controllers for other devices. In these roles, mini-computers will reduce teleprocessing traffic by placing substantial intelligence "outboard" from the central computer, and will improve the operation and cost-effectiveness of large, integrated applications.

Substantial growth will also occur in stand-alone minicomputers and microcomputers and in the many small, stand-alone applications suitable for these computers. Many such systems are in place today, and are successful and popular with their users. The applications run on these systems are small compared to the integrated applications run on large systems, are generally dependent only upon "local" data, and often serve single users or groups of users in the immediate area of the computer. Some of these systems are connected to large, central computers via communications lines to enable them to transfer information (be it data or decisions) to or from such central computers. We expect a major expansion in stand-alone minicomputers running such applications as stock or inventory control, text processing, etc. We return to this topic in Section 8 of Chapter 5.

The general class of applications known as "process control" is currently experiencing substantial growth; this trend will continue, and probably accelerate, in the future. Such factors as environmental controls, increasing costs of raw materials, increasing costs of utilities (heat, fuel, power, etc.) and the consequently increasing emphasis on process efficiency are all contributing to this growth. These systems will sometimes be stand-alone control systems, sometimes part of an interconnected computer hierarchy, and sometimes a combination operating primarily in stand-alone mode, but capable of being connected to a large computer to transfer to it operating results and to obtain from it operating guidelines.

5. POTENTIAL FOR HOME COMPUTER APPLICATIONS

The general idea of providing home data processing capabilities to the public has been a topic of speculation among information processing specialists for several years. The social value of home data processing is potentially enormous in terms of educational applications alone; if entertainment, games, and other applications are also considered, this social value is augmented by commercial desirability. At present, the potential market includes approximately 100 million homes in North America, Western Europe, and Japan; obviously, this is a large enough market to make the idea worth exploring. Two questions remain. Is it technologically feasible to provide this capability at a cost acceptable to the public? Can the concept be made sufficiently attractive to create among the public a feeling of need for the acquisition of such a capability? These questions are, of course, inextricably linked; they are the usual price and demand considerations.

The technological feasibility is unquestionable [Weisbecker 1974]; with a minicomputer, a substantial data processing capability can be provided at a cost approximating 10% of the cost of modest housing, less than the cost of a typical automobile, or something under twice the combined cost of a stove, a refrigerator, and a washing machine. (These examples are not gratuitous; the public generally purchases such items on credit, an arrangement well suited to the purchase of a home computer facility.) Unfortunately, however valuable the home computer might be as an educational tool, it is debatable whether large numbers of people would acquire it for that purpose alone. However, if it is presented as a home entertainment device with appeal to a broad spectrum of ages and interests, the public might well buy it. One major vehicle for attracting broad public interest in this concept can be found in the widespread popularity of games—Sears, Roebuck and Co. is already marketing a computer that enables one to play a version of ping-pong on a home TV set for just under one hundred dollars.

Two fundamentally distinct approaches to providing home data processing exist. The first is based on time-sharing, with large machines at central locations connected via communication links to home terminal devices. In commercial data processing applications, this makes sense, both structurally and economically. In the home environment, it is far less applicable. The cost of communications, the need to deal with the common carriers as intermediaries, and the necessary involvement of Federal regulation (e.g., via the FCC) are barriers that increase the appeal of the second approach, that of stand-alone processors employing minicomputers. The key factor is the radical reduction in the cost of substantial data processing capability. Table 4.1 (based on data from Theis and Hobbs [1969] and Hobbs and McLaughlin [1974]) shows the decreasing price trend of minicomputers since the introduction of 8K-byte machines in 1965 and of 4K-byte machines in 1969; these machines provide something like the data processing power of a 1960-vintage machine costing one million dollars.

TABLE 4.1

PRICE TREND OF MINICOMPUTERS
(In Thousands of Dollars)

Memory size	1965	1967	1969	1971	1973	1975
4K bytes	....	....	6.4	4.0	2.6	1.7
8K bytes	25.0	16.0	10.2	6.4	4.1	2.6

The figures in Table 4.1 are the unit prices for a single purchase in an environment in which the contemplated annual sales are on the order of, at best, a few thousand machines. In very large quantities, the price would, of course, be reduced by both manufacturing economies and bulk-order discounts. On the other hand, for the kind of systems contemplated here, other effects would increase the cost somewhat. For example, the prices quoted cover the arithmetic and control units, the high-speed storage unit of the given size, and a power supply between the wall plug and the computer. Additional hardware to interface with, perhaps, two or three tape-cassette or "floppy-disk" transports, a commercial television set, and one or more control boxes approximating the twelve- or sixteen-button telephone-like input device are likely to be required [Computer Decisions 1974; Weisbecker 1974]. Also, some kind of decorative packaging would be desirable for something that would doubtless be living room or den furniture. A reasonable working figure would be, initially, two thousand dollars for a complete system.

The current trends in this direction are twofold and come from opposite directions. First, of course, minicomputer costs are decreasing into this price range. Second, the functional capabilities of the "pocket" calculator are increasing. Programmable pocket calculators are now on the market for under two hundred dollars. Programs for such calculators can be developed by the user or purchased from vendors. These two trends are already converging toward the home data processing capability.

The home computer can be envisioned as an isolated system whose only connection with the outside world is through its use of electric power. However, given availability of the telephone network and the potential spread of two-way Cable Area Television (CATV) [Jones 1973], the possibility of connection to neighborhood or, eventually, worldwide networks opens another broad area of applications. The synergistic social effects of this possibility are awesome.

If the barriers to the availability of communications capabilities for the general-purpose home computer could be overcome, a whole new set of applications would become feasible, based on the combination of a home computer and an inexpensive communications capability (e.g., telephone, CATV) connected to central data bases. Home access to stock quotations and to other stock-market data (such as performance statistics of various corporations), libraries maintained in computer storage, and personal financial data (such as data on personal expenditures furnished by banks) bring to mind a large number of other potential applications [Dantzig and Saaty 1973].

6. CONCLUSIONS

The trends in data processing applications discussed in this chapter indicate that, in all segments of society where data processing applications originate today, such applications will grow into large, integrated sets of applications systems oriented toward on-line transaction processing, with heavy data-base and data communications requirements. There will also be significant growth in sensor-based applications. At the same time, the accelerating proliferation of stand-alone minicomputer-based systems will continue, with such systems serving as intelligent terminals in hierarchical computer networks and as increasingly practical and appealing devices for implementing "isolated" applications requiring only locally available data. The possible emergence of home computers may well generate a totally new, massive market for minicomputer applications in the 1980's.

REFERENCES

Boehm, B. W. 1973. Software and its impact: A quantitative assessment. *Datamation* **19**(5):48-59.

Computer Decisions. 1974. Home computers from RCA and DEC. *Computer Decisions* **6**(6):2.

Dantzig, G. B., and Saaty, T. L. 1973. *The compact city: A plan for a liveable urban environment.* San Francisco: W. H. Freeman.

Hobbs, L. C. and McLaughlin, R. A. 1974. Minicomputer survey. *Datamation* **20**(7):50-61.

Jones, M. V. 1973. How cable television may change our lives. *The Futurist* **7**(5):196-99.

Plugge, W. R., and Perry, M. N. 1961. American Airlines' "SABRE" electronic reservations system. *Proc. Western Joint Computer Conference,* vol. 19, pp. 593-601.

Theis, D. J. and Hobbs, L. C. 1969. Mini-computers for real-time applications. *Datamation* 15(3):39-61.

Weisbecker, J. 1974. A practical, low-cost, home/school microprocessor system. *Computer* 7(8):20-31.

Wylie, K. 1971. Summary of results: GUIDE/IBM study of advanced applications. 111 E. Wacker Dr., Chicago, IL 60601: GUIDE International.

5

HARDWARE

No amount of genius can overcome a
preoccupation with detail.

M. J. Levy, Jr.

1. INTRODUCTION

No study of the problems of the data processing industry would be complete without a discussion of data processing hardware. It is our opinion, however, that the problems of the data processing industry that are directly related to hardware are small as compared to problems in the other areas we consider. This chapter is included for the sake of completeness, rather than to thoroughly explore the potential hardware developments, or to illuminate some heretofore undiscovered problems attributable to hardware technology. Readers who are interested in a more complete forecast of data processing hardware developments should consult some of the many recent publications on this topic [Turn 1974; Greenblott and Hsiao 1975; Withington 1975; Hodges 1976].

The approach we take to forecasting the future of hardware is a deliberately conservative one. This is so for several reasons. First, "leading-edge" technology is not likely to have a significant impact on the mainstream of general-purpose data processing in the 1980-1985 time period because of the lengthening technology transfer time and of the generally prevailing conservative fiscal attitudes toward equipment replacement. Second, a prediction of a revolution in hardware architecture violates the basic ground rules of this study. Finally, we repeat our opinion that the lack of hardware capabilities is *not* the major constraining influence on the growth of our industry.

The preeminent fact about the data processing hardware that is likely to be available in 1985 is that the cost/performance ratio of that hardware will decrease very significantly from what it is today. This decrease will not be uniform. It is likely to range from a factor of 3 to 10 for peripherals, to a factor of 30 to 100 for main memory and central processors, to perhaps a factor of 300 to 1,000 for individual logic modules. The manufacturing cost/performance ratio for entire systems will, in all likelihood, continue to improve by roughly a factor of 10 every five years.

Of course, the actual savings to the end user will not be nearly as large as the raw decreases in the cost/performance ratio of the hardware. Additional functional sophistication, vendors' marketing and overhead costs, other (essentially fixed) costs such as power supplies, frames, "skins," etc., and, in particular, requirements for greatly increased reliability, will tend to consume a large proportion of the savings resulting from such cost/performance improvements. Furthermore, the hardware as delivered to the user often comes with some software (e.g., an operating system) which increases the price of that hardware. One must take care to avoid the confusion that can occur between manufacturing costs of hardware and its price to the purchaser. Many current hardware projections are *cost* projections, and the translation of such projections into prices or price/performance ratios is not obvious; prices depend on a very large number of factors, including the vendors' perception of the marketplace. We do expect that in 1985 users will get several times as much processing per dollar as they get today [Dennis and Smith 1972]. However, we also expect that the end users will require continually increasing amounts of data processing resources so that, in the end, the expenditures of a "typical" enterprise for hardware will continue to increase [Gilchrist and Weber 1973], and the rate of that increase may also grow.

The architecture of the *basic* hardware of general-purpose computers will, in all likelihood, not change drastically; however, the *apparent* functions (as seen by the users) that such computers will perform will be substantially changed and improved. Thus, we expect to see the reduction to practice of such capabilities as:

- speaker verification;
- speech understanding, i.e., understanding of (some) spoken words[1] and generation of appropriate responses;

---
1. Speech recognition (e.g., speech-driven typewriter) will not, in our opinion, become a commercial reality by 1985.

- handwritten text recognition (via graphic tablets, scanners, etc.);
- ability to use a human finger as a data pointer (like a light pen);
- high-quality synthetic speech.

In addition, the quantity, flexibility, and reliability of digital data communications, including such facilities as switched digital data networks, packet communications, much wider bandwidths, etc., will increase greatly [Roberts 1973; Roberts 1974; Allan 1975; Falk 1975; Moster and Pamm 1975; Mennie 1976].

It is virtually certain that logic modules—up to whole mini- or microcomputers—will appear as integral, built-in components in a wide variety of applications. Microcomputers may well appear in construction equipment (e.g., bulldozers), trucks, automobiles (e.g., non-skid brake systems), autonomous traffic control signals, and even in home appliances (e.g., dishwashers) [Winder 1976], just as minicomputers are used today in aircraft navigation systems.

There will be decreases in physical size and power consumption of most hardware *components* (but *not* necessarily of entire computer systems). An exception to this will be human-directed input/output devices, whose speed (for interactive devices) and size are ultimately tied to the speed and size of human beings (e.g., the wave of hand-held calculators appears to have reached the limit of miniaturization of buttons meant to be actuated by the fingers of average adults.) There will be little if any growth (and perhaps a shrinkage) in card-oriented peripheral devices. Printers will get faster, and non-impact printers will become more common.

It is important to note that *reliability, availability,* and *security* will assume extreme importance and will, in all likelihood, become dominant criteria. Thus, for instance, whenever design trade-off questions arise between, say, an increase in reliability versus a decrease in size or power consumption, the increase in reliability will be chosen in almost all cases.

2. RELIABILITY, AVAILABILITY, AND MAINTENANCE

As more enterprises begin to rely more heavily on data processing systems for their day-to-day operations, the problems of reliability, availability, and maintenance are rapidly gaining importance, to the point where reliability and availability are becoming (and in some instances already have become) the primary concern of users [Marcus 1974].

Achieving acceptable reliability and availability is one of the major problems the data processing industry faces. By 1985, users will demand a level of reliability comparable to that achieved by the No. 1 ESS telephone central offices, which are currently averaging one hour of downtime every four years [Clement et al. 1974]; this represents an improvement by a factor of more than 100 over the reliability and availability of today's large, general-purpose systems. In this context, we are speaking of the reliability of the *entire system:* central processor, storage, peripherals, microcode, operating system, applications programs, data bases, etc.

Certain trends in user demands are already discernible:

- willingness to trade *instantaneous* computing power for *sustained* power;
- need for disaster backup facilities designed into the system from the start;
- willingness to trade infrequent, very long outages for *somewhat* more frequent (but *not* clustered) very short outages (i.e., the mean time to repair is, in some cases, a more crucial concern than the mean time to failure; this is especially true of on-line applications);
- great fear of the potentially catastrophic event best described by the expression "the data base is down";
- willingness to pay for environmental aids to reliability: "uninterruptible" power supplies; better air conditioning, dust, and humidity controls; site security and hardening; etc.;
- concern about reliability of *access* to data that resides in hierarchical, distributed, and virtual storage spaces (i.e., when only the system knows where the data is);
- need for graceful degradation and fail-soft capabilities.

Of course, reliability and availability have their price, in terms both of dollars and of performance. But while the problem of increasing *hardware* reliability is essentially an economic issue, its solution is inadequate without solving the *total system* reliability problem, and it is not clear that the problem of *software* reliability can be solved with money alone. We do feel that there are already sufficient economic incentives and pressures to force the industry into an all-out attack on this larger problem. On the other hand, we do not, today, see a ready solution. We perceive a great deal of concern for the problem, but no concrete means to convert this concern into meaningful solutions. The industry's "track record" in this area is quite poor, and even in hardware, several approaches that were tried have backfired. For instance, use of parity checking in IBM System/360 computers has not markedly improved the reliability of that series of computers (there are those who claim it has actually decreased it, by causing machine errors due solely to the parity checking mechanisms). As another example, some users claim that many IBM 370/168's had, as of the end of 1973, a lower overall reliability record than IBM 360/65's. One way for users to attack the reliability and availability problem is to provide a strong incentive for the vendors to behave as if their revenues were directly proportional to the reliability and availability of their systems.

Hardware maintenance will become much more standardized and mechanized (i.e., automated); diagnosis will become much more centralized. Much of the maintenance will be done by independent ("outboard") minicomputers or by remote diagnostic centers. The effort will be centered on isolating and replacing the one malfunctioning *major functional* unit (e.g., on the order of 1% or 2%, or even a larger fraction of the central processor or memory); this will be made possible by large scale integration (LSI) devices consisting of over 10,000 gates *per chip,* with 100 or more chips per plug-in unit [Greenblott and Hsiao 1975]. Error detection, error correction, and fault-tolerant circuitry will assist in the task, as will the significant increases in the inherent reliability of devices, circuits, and subsystems. There will be widespread use of on-line monitoring and diagnostic capabilities, with automatic retry and path switching. Despite security problems, remote dial-up diagnosis will also spread. Almost all, if not all, engineering changes and repairs will take place at the factory, with replacements for "pluggable" subsystems shipped to the customer site. The customer engineer will become an expert at *replacing* modules and components while the system is up. The problems of maintaining multiple-vendor systems will become more severe. This will create a business opportunity for independent hardware maintenance firms.

One aspect of maintenance that is a severe problem results from the fact that there has been a gradual increase in the mean time to *failure* (or to "cold start") of data processing systems, but without a corresponding decrease in the mean time to *repair* (and, occasionally, at the cost of an *increase* in the mean time to repair). The repairability of data processing systems must be improved; it is not enough to construct them so that they break down less often. When the inevitable failure does occur, it must be contained in such a way that minimal damage occurs to the total system. We expect that home computers of the type discussed in Section 5 of Chapter 4 will be very reliable, and whatever maintenance they require will be provided in a manner similar to today's repair of television sets and office typewriters, with the emphasis again being on replacing failing modules that are subsequently repaired at the factory or at a regional repair center.

In summary, the industry must aim for a level of total system reliability and availability that is high enough to make these secondary, rather than primary, concerns on the part of users. We give some quantitative data on reliability in Appendix B.

3. CENTRAL PROCESSORS AND LOGIC

We foresee dramatic reductions in the costs of central processing units (CPUs) on a "per executed instruction" basis [Dennis and Smith 1972], and significant reductions on a "function performed" basis. The basic machine clock cycle may well go below ten nanoseconds [Ware 1972].

CPU architecture will change, but not so radically that it will make obsolete the accumulated knowledge and understanding of the "traditional" CPU architecture. More and more sophistication will appear in the form of functions and capabilities implemented in microcode. There will be much more use made of advanced CPU architectural forms (including coupled and distributed CPUs) to deal with specific problems of speed of processing, data organization, etc. More sophisticated interrupt structures, architecture directed towards associative and multilevel memories, and multilevel paging and swapping techniques will become more commonplace. We consider all of these to be expected extensions of today's state of the art in CPU architecture, and we no longer view them as new developments.

The present growth in the use of LSI will continue to exert very strong pressures to provide more and more logic in terminals, control units, channels, etc. These devices will tend, by becoming more and more independently capable, to assume more and more of the control, housekeeping, and other non-arithmetic responsibilities currently performed by CPUs. This trend could cause, as a side effect, some unexpected security problems [Attanasio, Markstein, and Phillips 1976].

The microcomputer-on-a-chip [Rudenberg 1972] will proliferate in many guises; we have alluded to this phenomenon in Section 1 above.

4. STORAGE

Multilevel hierarchical storage systems (with the hierarchy very likely hidden from the user) will become a reality by 1985. Virtual addressing schemes (with very large address spaces—perhaps as large as 10^{12} bytes, or even larger) will become dominant. "Automatic" data migration will tend to move frequently used data into "higher" (i.e., faster) levels of storage, and vice versa. There will exist at least the following levels of storage:

- "cache";
- primary;
- secondary;
- archival;
- disaster backup.

Each of these major levels may (and probably will) be further subdivided according to speed, access time, and cost considerations.

Data will leave the system only by being archived or discarded, or by being transported (by whatever means) to another (disjoint) system. We anticipate a strong trend to keep all data on-line, except for disaster backup copies and archival storage; and even for archival data, we expect that, as time passes, there will be a trend to keep more and more of it on-line.

4.1. Primary and Cache Storage

Much of what we said above on the topics of cost, speed, reliability, size, and power consumption applies to random-access read/write memories. We expect memory capacities to increase significantly, so that we may well see a single computer accessing a (real) main memory containing up to 10^9 bytes. Multiple-error correction will become an absolute necessity of memory design (this will also apply to lower levels of storage). Because of the very large real address spaces available (not to mention the even larger virtual address spaces), novel and more sophisticated addressing schemes will be needed. Dynamic address translation, relocation, segmentation, and paging (with both fixed and variable page sizes) are already common. Cache memories, in a variety of sizes and speeds, will be more widely used, at least as long as they maintain substantial speed and economic advantages over main memories.

4.2. Secondary Storage

The trend toward large data-base applications will force an explosive growth in on-line secondary devices. A number of so-called "mass-storage" devices already exist, but they have not yet become commonplace; we expect that their popularity will grow. The variety of available densities, access times, and transfer rates will grow. The predominant storage technology will continue to utilize magnetic and electromechanical devices: disks, drums, etc. Tape usage will grow much more slowly and may, in fact, already be peaking out. Tape cassettes and "diskettes" will become commonplace as adjuncts to remote terminals. The cost per byte of all of these devices will continue to decrease significantly. Hardware data compression capabilities will make more efficient use of secondary storage. For example, the overall economics will in all likelihood make it less costly to store text on-line than to print it.

Memories based on magnetic bubbles [Bobeck, Bonyhard, and Geusic 1975; Ypma 1975], holographic techniques [Gillis, Hoffman, and Nelson 1975], and Josephson devices [Anacker 1975] will appear, but will not become predominant until sometime after 1985. (Magnetic bubble *logic* [Chang, Chen, and Tung 1973] may also prove economically feasible, but somewhat after bubble memories.) As for cost, there are already those who envisage mass memories at a cost of 10^{-6} cent/bit [Davis 1973]. This is approximately what magnetic tape costs today (on a per-bit basis), *not* including the cost of access (drives, channels, etc.); today, such costs of access are approximately a factor of 100 larger than the cost of the tape itself. We foresee the emergence (perhaps after 1985) of image or picture storage (e.g., for storing actual image copies of checks, insurance policies, credit slips, etc., rather than storing their text; such image copies may well acquire legal standing, unlike digitally stored text), with associated video retrieval, scan, and display facilities.

It is probable that, especially in large systems, there will be several levels of secondary storage; it is likely, however, that the users (especially the mid users and the end users) will not need to be aware of this fact.

4.3. Archival and Disaster Backup Storage

The growth in primary and secondary storage will mandate an equally impressive growth in archival storage. Ideally, archival storage should retain information essentially forever without requiring any power, be inexpensive, have good handling properties, and be physically immune to any failures that might destroy its contents. It usually does not have to be accessed rapidly, but it must be reliable. At present, we do not know of any materials that possess all these qualities to an adequate degree.

Neither magnetic tape (including videotape) nor microfilm (as it is used today) offers long-term solutions to the problem of archival storage. Tape is basically an off-line storage medium. The shelf-life of the information stored on tape is not very good (and often not predictable a priori) because of bleed-through and other problems [Gentile 1973]. Archival storage is typically written once and read an arbitrary number of times. The ability to rewrite magnetic tape is not a great advantage in the context of archival storage; in fact, because of the danger of erasure, tape presents a definite *disadvantage* in this case. Microfilm, holograms, and any other inexpensive write-once, read-many-times media are preferable from this point of view.

Microfilm, today, is used primarily in data processing applications to store printed (non-graphic) matter in reduced size, as a substitute for paper. The expected reduction in on-line storage costs may well make this type of microfilm usage much less attractive. We note, however, that potential developments in holographic storage, image storage, gray-scale and full-color non-calligraphic displays, etc., may make good use of microfilm technology. In these applications, information on microfilm will be stored in a denser form than is the case today, and will *not*, in all likelihood, be directly readable by humans, since the information will probably be encoded (and redundant—as in a hologram). For microfilm to become truly useful as an archival storage medium (especially for on-line archival storage), methods that allow microfilm records to be retrieved, read, and sorted by machines will have to be developed.

Today, the entire problem of archival storage has no known satisfactory solution. The need for such a solution is very pressing, and we believe this pressure will force many new developments in the next ten years, one or more of which may provide an adequate solution.

Disaster backup storage is, by definition, an off-line form of storage. It shares all of the requirements of archival storage except that it does not have quite as stringent a longevity requirement. Therefore, magnetic tape will probably continue to be used for disaster backup somewhat further into the future than for other forms of storage. With time, disaster backup is very likely to become simply a form of off-line archival storage.

5. TELEPROCESSING AND INPUT/OUTPUT CONTROLLERS

Teleprocessing and input/output controllers will become more independently capable and more self-sufficient. By this we mean that, little by little, the industry will get away from the concept that "the CPU is the master, and the peripherals (including humans) are its slaves." Gradually, the CPU's responsibility will become to *respond* to peripheral requests. This concept was pioneered in, among others, the CDC 6600, continued by the UNIVAC 1100 series and the GE 635/645, and can often be found today in minicomputers. IBM has not made much use of this concept in their main-line commercial equipment (the IBM 1800 and System/7 being minor exceptions). More and more of the input/output functions (e.g., message switching) will be handled with essentially no "traditional" CPU intervention. Automatic data compression and decompression may well be done by secondary storage input/output controllers, or within terminal devices themselves.

Input/output controllers, teleprocessing controllers, multiplexors, concentrators, and even "modems" will continue to become more and more independent, self-checking, and asynchronous in their relations with the CPU. Teleprocessing controllers will be much more tolerant of baud rates and line disciplines, and much more able to cope with transmission errors. Encrypting and decrypting (much of it in hardware) will become much more common than it is today.

6. COMMUNICATIONS FACILITIES

Long-haul data communication is becoming less expensive. The whole topic of communications facilities is, obviously, not only a technical subject, but one with very strong legal and regulatory overtones [Walker 1972; Strassburg 1973]. Growth of such facilities is very strongly dependent on the availability of capital [La Blanc and Himsworth 1972]. The distinctions between "data communications," "data processing," and "message switching" are becoming increasingly blurred. So are the questions raised by international, national, and private satellites. Some projections are, nevertheless, possible. AT&T's

Digital Data System® (DDS)—with hot standby channels—will expand into a truly nationwide network before the end of the 1970's [Moster and Pamm 1975]; a similar service already exists in Canada. It will significantly reduce costs of large-volume, long-haul data transmission. A *switched* DDS may well follow.

Transmission rates of around 50,000 baud will become prevalent, with some corresponding atrophy in the 1,000 to 10,000 baud range. By 1985, costs for large-volume data transmission may decrease by as much as a factor of ten. Packet communications are beginning to appear [Ornstein et al. 1972; Abramson 1973; Roberts 1974]. We are, as yet, uncertain about the degree of acceptance they will get. The cost of satellite links (not including ground connections) will also go down significantly, especially for long-haul (e.g., intercontinental) routes. The number of ground stations will go up and their cost will go down, reducing the cost of ground connections. Optical transmission media (e.g., glass fiber lightguides) are in experimental use today. By 1985, they promise to further reduce the costs and increase the reliability of data transmission.

All of these developments will clearly benefit users of large-volume, high-usage data transmission routes. Local connections ("local loop") will, however, remain a problem, and costs here are not likely to decrease a great deal. Thus, the cost to transmit 5 or 10 million bytes per hour, 24 hours a day, day in and day out, will go down significantly; but to collect sales data from 10,000 gasoline pumps in real time will still be very expensive by present methods. Extensive use of multiplexing and concentration will help but will not solve the problem. Sophisticated hardware error correction and retry capabilities will be required and will be expensive. Regional data collection and processing "utilities" may appear. They will face some very difficult legal and regulatory problems, in addition to the technological and competitive ones.

There will exist very high bandwidth (above 10^7 baud) data-transmission facilities, but primarily for specialized applications. Facilities up to 10^6 baud will be more common. Just how common they will become depends partially on whether cable television (CATV) becomes a truly nationwide facility with a two-way transmission capability that can carry digital (in addition to analog) messages [Falk 1975]. As an adjunct, it is interesting to speculate on whether CATV will be allowed to carry two-way, low baud-rate digital signals for use with home data terminals [Jones 1973].

What is certain is that, by 1985, a large fraction of the signals carried by the U.S. telephone network will be digital. This will make data communications easier and less expensive; it will also decrease transmission errors significantly.

Problems of line protocols and their current inefficiencies and incompatibilities (half or full duplex, start-stop or synchronous, EBCDIC or ASCII, line turn-around, hand-shaking, etc.) will be resolved to increase throughput and compatibility. The recently introduced Synchronous Data Link Control (SDLC) discipline [Donnan and Kersey 1974] is a first attempt in that direction.

7. TERMINALS

While the cost of terminals will decrease, we do not believe that this decrease will be dramatic. We predict that, instead of a dramatic cost decrease, we are likely to see terminals become more "capable" and faster, and to embody features such as automatic text compression and decompression, selective transmission of text (to save on communication costs—this trend can already be recognized in terminals such as the IBM 3270), automatic error correction in modems (which will often be directly built into terminals), automatic retry in case of error, higher baud rates, etc. In addition, the following broad predictions can be made regarding terminals:

• Their number will grow exponentially. In recent years, the terminal sector of the data processing industry has been growing at a rate significantly higher than that of the industry as a whole, and we expect this trend to continue [Salzman 1975].
• Their variety will also grow very markedly.
• They will replace many office typewriters and some other office machines.
• They will range in complexity from Touch-Tone® telephones to medium-size computers.
• The "simple" versus "intelligent" terminal distinction will blur, but the trend will be to more and more capability ("intelligence").
• There will be a much larger proportion of terminals with character-display [Granholm 1976] and graphic capabilities, as opposed to the hard-copy-only devices [Granholm 1975]. But there is still room for major improvement in hard-copy terminals, including interactive [Dolotta 1970] as well as "batch" terminals.

- Graphic *output* terminals will become much more common than they are today.
- Graphic *input* terminals will become a commercial reality, even though graphic input is much more expensive today than graphic output. This disparity may decrease somewhat by 1985.
- There will be more and more specialized terminals—for point-of-sale, assembly-line reporting, banking, airline reservations, data entry and capture, text preparation, typesetting, etc. The many applications based on such specialized terminals will begin replacing some optical character-recognition (OCR) applications, with a corresponding reduction in the rate of growth of the OCR sector of the data processing industry.
- The use of voice response will become much more common than it is today.
- Voice *input* capability has already appeared, but even by 1985, it will still be in an experimental stage.
- We may see a much wider acceptance of hand-held terminals [Roberts 1972].
- It will be a rare computer that is not, at some time or another, a terminal to another system.
- The more versatile remote batch "terminals" will, in turn, be able to support interactive terminals, etc.

As far as cost is concerned, a minimal hard-copy terminal will cost about twice as much as a portable electric typewriter, while the cost of a character display terminal will approach asymptotically the cost of a portable color television receiver.

The emergence of a *home* terminal market will depend on a variety of factors; we discussed some of these factors in Section 5 of Chapter 4. The following are some of the prerequisites for the emergence of such a market:

- adequate (in both quality and cost) communications facilities;
- adequate reliability and means of maintenance;
- local (to the terminal) storage facilities;
- existence of publicly accessible data bases containing information of interest to the end users of home terminals;
- software which is specifically tailored to make home terminals usable by (and useful to) such users.

The potential market for home terminals is, of course, enormous, provided that the above prerequisites can be satisfied.

8. MICRO-, MINI-, MIDI-, AND MAXICOMPUTERS

Mini- and microcomputer usage will continue its explosive growth [Hollingworth 1973; Nelson 1975; Coury 1976]. Much use of these processors will occur inside other devices (in a dedicated manner), e.g., in input/output controllers, terminals, calculators, automobiles, etc., as was pointed out in Section 1 above. Minicomputers will also be used for a large variety of stand-alone applications (see Section 4 of Chapter 4), including an ever increasing number of process-control applications [Business Week 1973]; in fact, they will be used wherever they offer a cost advantage or added convenience over larger computers. We repeat here the point made in Section 1.4 of Chapter 1, namely that the conclusions of this study are independent of the rate of growth in the numbers of minicomputers, as opposed to the rate of growth of the number of large, general-purpose computers.

Mini- and microcomputers will penetrate the home market, disguised, at first, as hand calculators [Mennie 1974], games [Weisbecker 1974], "home systems" (e.g., fire detection, security, appliance controllers) [Winder 1976], etc., as discussed in Section 5 of Chapter 4.

On the other end of the minicomputer scale, there already exist "midicomputers" (e.g., a PDP 11/70, which, in a large configuration, may cost over 100,000 dollars and offers processing and data storage capabilities significantly in excess of what the Compatible Time-Sharing System (CTSS) [Corbató et al. 1963] offered in 1965 on a very large IBM 7094). And, of course, the very large (including some one-of-a-kind) maxicomputers will get much faster. Thus, the spectrum of sizes and processing capabilities will expand at both ends of the scale.

9. HARDWARE, FIRMWARE, AND SOFTWARE

There exists a clear trend toward more and more extensive use of "firmware" (microcoding) to implement functions that previously were hard-wired or, in some instances, performed by software. Thus, the complexity of hard-wired logic is still increasing, but not as fast as the complexity of the "machine language" which is seen by the software; the latter is becoming more and more "sophisticated" and "higher-level." We expect that more and more functions previously performed by software will be implemented in microcode (e.g., parts of paging, data access, and interrupt mechanisms, as well as higher-level language interpreters or parts thereof).

We must stress, however, that there is no magic in firmware. It shares many of the problems of both software and hardware, even though it does have many distinct advantages of its own: it is easier to modify (but slower) than hardware, and faster (but harder to modify) than software. It does add flexibility to the design process, and has thus become another tool for the computer designer [Mandell 1972]. Programs implemented in firmware are *not* inherently more reliable than their software counterparts; it is just that, in the past, when firmware was very hard to modify, there was a greater incentive to "debug" programs implemented in firmware more completely before installing them. (Additionally, such programs, in the past, tended to be small and simple, and thus easier to "debug.") The advent of "writable" firmware has removed much of this incentive.

We believe that more use will be made of firmware, but that, in the great majority of cases, users will have little, if any, access to it because of very strong counter-pressures resulting from the reliability and maintenance problems that such access creates.

10. COMPUTER NETWORKS

Computers can be linked into networks in several configurations, e.g., star, ring, point-to-point, hierarchical [Anderson and Jensen 1975]. They can communicate using either message-switching or store-and-forward techniques (packet and others), via conventional communications facilities, via satellites, etc. Although the number of conceivable distinct configurations is extremely large, the industry's ability to properly design, install, and manage networks is, today, minimal, because there exists, to date, very little experience with computer networks [Pyke and Blanc 1973]. We distinguish, in this context, *computer* networks (i.e., networks consisting of several *cooperating*—but essentially independent—computers) from *telecommunication* networks and remote-access data processing facilities, such as remote job entry, time-sharing, various on-line and real-time systems, etc. Computer networks seem to offer a number of very appealing *potential* advantages [Roberts and Wessler 1970; Bell 1974]:

- load sharing;
- resource sharing;
- data transfer;
- high degree of (at least partial) survivability;

- graceful degradation;
- economies of scale;
- access to large numbers of data bases;
- process and data distribution.

On the other hand, for computer networks to become commercially viable, a number of problems will have to be solved [Enslow 1973]. Many of these problems exist in all computer systems, but they tend to become more severe in the context of computer networks, e.g.:

- security and "auditability";
- reliability and cost effectiveness of communication links;
- standardization of data formats, communication protocols, user protocols, operating procedures, etc.;
- availability of adequate disaster backup;
- thorough understanding of the basic concepts of data and process distribution.

We believe that, between now and 1985, there will be significant growth in computer networks, but we do not believe that they will become the predominant data processing way of life in that time period. We expect remote-access facilities to grow at a much faster rate than computer networks. We discuss computer networks from a different point of view in Section 5.4 of Chapter 6.

11. CONCLUSIONS

By 1985, the percentage of the total direct data processing dollar[2] spent on hardware will decrease to between 15% and 25% from today's level of 25% to 45% [McLaughlin 1976]. On the other hand, total expenditures for *hardware* will continue to grow, and may well double by 1985[3] [Gilchrist and Weber 1973]. This implies that total data processing expenditures may quadruple over that period (see Table B.1 of Appendix B). Thus, in a typical large business enterprise, the fraction of gross revenues spent for data processing will more than double— assuming that gross revenues, on the average, grow roughly in proportion to the GNP (see Table A.2 of Appendix A). That fraction already runs as high as 3% for some industries, but somewhat lower than 0.5%

---

2. Which does not include *all* of the money spent on data processing, because some costs (e.g., salaries of end users) are very often not identified as data processing expenses [McLaughlin 1976].

3. We deal here with constant ("inflation-proof") dollars.

for others. The growth in data processing expenditures will be slower in mature industries than in newer ones.

The percentage of hardware dollars expended on terminals, communication facilities, and teleprocessing controllers will increase, on the average, to over 40% of the total [Dennis and Smith 1972; Salzman 1975]. The particular ratios that will apply in various situations will be strongly influenced by the then current trade-offs between transmission and processing costs. Thus, if overall processing costs fall much more sharply than overall communications costs, then the growth in communications-based data processing will be slower, and vice versa. For comparison, we note that today, many large installations spend about 10% of their hardware dollars on terminals and communications; such communications facilities are often also used for voice and teletypewriter communications, in addition to data communications. We also expect that, in most installations, the cost of peripherals and of secondary and archival storage will significantly outweigh the cost of central processors and of primary storage.

The rate at which communications-based data processing will grow (including networks of computers) is also dependent upon the bigger issue of the distribution of data processing power (centralized versus decentralized data processing). This last issue presents some very complex problems[4] with managerial, administrative, and "political" overtones, and, in addition, has a number of genuinely technological problems associated with it. The growth of data-base applications [Wylie 1971] will push toward centralization until and unless the problems of distributed data bases and computer networks are solved in a commercially viable fashion.

REFERENCES

Abramson, N. 1973. Packet switching with satellites. *Proc. AFIPS National Computer Conference,* vol. 42, pp. 695-702.

Allan, R. 1975. Components. *IEEE Spectrum* 12(4):56-59.

Anacker, W. 1975. Superconducting memories employing Josephson devices. *Proc. AFIPS National Computer Conference,* vol. 44, pp. 529-34.

Anderson, G. A., and Jensen, E. D. 1975. Computer interconnection structures: Taxonomy, characteristics, and examples. *Computing Surveys* 7(4):197-213.

Attanasio, C. R., Markstein, P. W., and Phillips, R. J. 1976. Penetrating an operating system: A study of VM/370 integrity. *IBM Systems Journal* 15(1):102-16.

---

4. Which we also touch upon in Sections 1 and 4 of Chapter 7.

Bell, C. G. 1974. More power by networking. *IEEE Spectrum* 11(2):40-45.

Bobeck, A. H., Bonyhard, P. I., and Geusic, J. E. 1975. Magnetic bubbles: An emerging new memory technology. *Proc. IEEE* 63(8):1176-95.

Business Week. 1973. Minicomputers that run the factory. *Business Week,* No. 2309, December 8, 1973, pp. 68-78.

Chang, H., Chen, T. C., and Tung, C. 1973. The realization of symmetric switching functions using magnetic bubble technology. *Proc. AFIPS National Computer Conference,* vol. 42, pp. 413-20.

Clement, G. F., Jones, W. C., and Watters, R. J. 1974. No. 1 ESS processors: How dependable have they been? *Bell Laboratories Record* 52(1):21-25.

Corbató, F. J., Daggett, M. M., Daley, R. C., Creasy, R, J., Hellwig, J. D., Orenstein, R. H., and Korn, L. K. 1963. *The compatible time-sharing system: A programmer's guide.* Cambridge, MA: M.I.T. Press.

Coury, F. F., ed. 1976. Special issue on microcomputers. *Computer* 9(1).

Davis, J. C. 1973. $10^{-5}-10^{-7}$ cent/bit storage media, what does it mean? *Proc. AFIPS National Computer Conference,* vol. 42, p. 518.

Dennis, S. F., and Smith, M. G. 1972. LSI: Implications for future design and architecture. *Proc. AFIPS Spring Joint Computer Conference,* vol. 40, pp. 343-51.

Dolotta, T. A. 1970. Functional specifications for typewriter-like time-sharing terminals. *Computing Surveys* 2(1):5-31.

Donnan, R. A., and Kersey, J. R. 1974. Synchronous data link control: A perspective. *IBM Systems Journal* 13(2):140-62.

Enslow, P. H., Jr. 1973. Non technical issues in network design: Economic, legal, social, and other considerations. *Computer* 6(8):21-30.

Falk, H. 1975. Communications. *IEEE Spectrum* 12(4):42-45.

Gentile, R. B. 1973. On the reading of very old magnetic tapes. *Datamation* 19(10):59-62.

Gilchrist, B., and Weber, R. E. 1973. *The state of the computer industry in the United States: Data for 1971 and projections for 1976.* Montvale, NJ 07645: American Federation of Information Processing Societies.

Gillis, A. K., Hoffmann, G. E., and Nelson, R. H. 1975. Holographic memories: Fantasy or reality? *Proc. AFIPS National Computer Conference,* vol. 44, pp. 535-39.

Granholm, J. W. 1975. Interactive hardcopy terminals. *Datamation* 21(11):51-60.

———. 1976. Alphanumeric display terminals. *Datamation* 22(1):40-52.

Greenblott, B. J., and Hsiao, M. Y. 1975. Where is technology taking us in data processing systems? *Proc. AFIPS National Computer Conference,* vol. 44, pp. 623-28.

Hodges, D. A. 1976. Trends in computer hardware technology. *Computer Design* 15(2):77-85.

Hollingworth, D. 1973. Minicomputers: A review of current technology, systems, and applications. Report R-1279. Santa Monica, CA 90406: Rand Corp.

Jones, M. V. 1973. How cable television may change our lives. *The Futurist* 7(5):196-99.

La Blanc, R. E., and Himsworth, W. E. 1972. Data communications in 1980: A capital market view. *Proc. AFIPS Spring Joint Computer Conference,* vol. 40, pp. 611-16.

McLaughlin, R. A. 1976. 1976 dp budget. *Datamation* 22(2):52-58.

Mandell, R. L. 1972. Hardware/software trade-offs: Reasons and directions. *Proc. AFIPS Fall Joint Computer Conference,* vol. 41, pt. I, pp. 453-59.

Marcus, M. J. 1974. On attaining the availability required in future information processing systems. *Information Processing 1974 (Proc. IFIP Congress 1974),* pp. 141-46. Amsterdam: North-Holland.

Mennie, D. 1974. The big roundup of small calculators. *IEEE Spectrum* 11(4):34-41.

―――. 1976. Communications: Electronics and optics, too. *IEEE Spectrum* 13(1):57-61.

Moster, C. R., and Pamm, L. R. 1975. The Digital Data System launches a new era in data communications. *Bell Laboratories Record* 53(11):421-26.

Nelson, J. C. 1975. The economic implications of microprocessors on future computer technology and systems. *Proc. AFIPS National Computer Conference,* vol. 44, pp. 629-32.

Ornstein, S. M., Heart, F. E., Crowther, W. R., Rising, H. K., Russell, S. B., and Michel, A. 1972. The terminal IMP for the ARPA computer network. *Proc. AFIPS Spring Joint Computer Conference,* vol. 40, pp. 243-54.

Pyke, T. N., Jr., and Blanc, R. P. 1973. Computer networking technology: A state of the art review. *Computer* 6(8):13-19.

Roberts, L. G. 1972. Extension of packet communication technology to a hand held personal terminal. *Proc. AFIPS Spring Joint Computer Conference,* vol. 40, pp. 295-98.

―――. 1973. Dynamic allocation of satellite capacity through packet reservation. *Proc. AFIPS National Computer Conference,* vol. 42, pp. 711-16.

―――. 1974. Data by the packet. *IEEE Spectrum* 11(2):46-51.

―――, and Wessler, B. D. 1970. Computer network development to achieve resource sharing. *Proc. AFIPS Spring Joint Computer Conference,* vol. 36, pp. 543-49.

Rudenberg, H. G. 1972. Approaching the minicomputer on a silicon chip: Progress and expectations for LSI circuits. *Proc. AFIPS Spring Joint Computer Conference,* vol. 40, pp. 775-81.

Salzman, R. M. 1975. The computer terminal industry: A forecast. *Datamation* 21(11):46-50.

Strassburg, B. 1973. Remarks before the 1973 National Computer Conference's Panel on Regulation of the Computer and Communications Industry. Session handout. June 4, 1973.

Turn, R. 1974. *Computers in the 1980s.* New York: Columbia Univ. Press.

Walker, P. M. 1972. Regulatory developments in data communications: The past five years. *Proc. AFIPS Spring Joint Computer Conference,* vol. 40, pp. 593-609.

Ware, W. H. 1972. The ultimate computer. *IEEE Spectrum* 9(3):84-91.

Weisbecker, J. 1974. A practical, low-cost, home/school microprocessor system. *Computer* 7(8):20-31.

Winder, R. O. 1976. Microprocessors in consumer markets. *Computer* 9(1):39-40.

Withington, F. G. 1975. Beyond 1984: A technology forecast. *Datamation* 21(1):54-73.

Wylie, K. 1971. Summary of results: GUIDE/IBM study of advanced applications. 111 E. Wacker Dr., Chicago, IL 60601: GUIDE International.

Ypma, J. E. 1975. Bubble domain memory systems. *Proc. AFIPS National Computer Conference,* vol. 44, pp. 523-28.

6

SOFTWARE

*When you can measure what you are
speaking about, and express it in numbers,
you know something about it; but when
you cannot measure it, when you cannot
express it in numbers, your knowledge is
of a meager and unsatisfactory kind: it
may be the beginning of knowledge, but
you have scarcely, in your thoughts,
advanced to the stage of science.*

Wm. Thomson, Lord Kelvin

1. INTRODUCTION

This chapter is principally concerned with how software is created to implement the applications that are described in Chapter 4 and that have the necessary qualities discussed in Chapter 3; for without software, a general-purpose computer is a useless collection of electronic and electromechanical components: it can do no useful work for its users. Software, then, is the element upon which automation and computerization are most heavily dependent. Unfortunately, it is also the least understood aspect of data processing systems.

For the purposes of this study, we define software as the collection of programs (however initially created and subsequently translated, linked, etc.) that are executed by the hardware. Software is the intangible, active element, either resident in or added to the computer's hardware, that controls and mediates the actions of the hardware so that the hardware performs those logical and arithmetic manipulations upon input data that produce the result desired by the user. (The words "program" and "software" are often used interchangeably, but the former often refers to a single unit in a collection of software.)

In its active state, software is intangible and invisible to its users and developers; a representation of software in its static state is the only one that can be observed and manipulated. The results of its actions upon data may be observed and tabulated, but the processes that software performs, the actions it takes, and the decisions it makes can only be inferred. This creates many problems for both the developers and users of software.

Software can be divided into two broad general classes: *system* software and *applications* software. System software is that set of programs whose primary function is to manage and control the physical and logical resources of a data processing system and to provide centralized utility functions. One of the more important components of system software is the system control program (SCP), about which more will be said later.

System software does little, if any, useful work *directly* on behalf of the end user. Software that does work in direct support of the end user is called applications software. Applications software covers the gamut of things for which data processing systems are best known, from designing nuclear reactors to producing periodic bills and statements.

Software is the product of programmers and has been a "problem" since the beginning of the computer era; but the nature and magnitude of the software problem have changed over time. In the early 1950's, when the number of computers was very small and the problems to which they were applied were limited, the primary problem of programmers, and therefore of software, was the difficulty of producing workable programs with the primitive tools and techniques that were then available. The invention, successively, of symbolic assemblers, higher-level languages, operating systems, and time-sharing provided needed help in many areas during those early days. In the late 1960s, after more than a decade of astounding growth for the data processing industry, it was believed that if the then estimated 100,000 programmers in the United States could not satisfy the demand for software, adding 50,000 more programmers was the solution to the problem [Bylinsky 1967]. Today, the perception is quite different. In the 1974 National Computer Conference keynote address [Glaser 1974], the president of the American Federation of Information Processing Societies accused the data processing industry of ignoring the growing inability of the programming profession to produce enough good software. His entire address was devoted to "the software problem." Many participants at that and other recent conferences expressed deep concern over the continued rising cost of software and the general lack of competence of many programmers.

Many of the perceived problems stem directly from the explosive growth of the data processing industry. This growth is responsible not only for the problems but also for confounding many attempts to solve them. Before a problem can be solved, it must first be clearly stated so that it is understandable to those charged with solving it; and in order to evaluate the worth of a proposed solution, one must be able to determine how that solution will change things. This implies some sense of history. The data processing industry can at best only guess where it has been and where it is today. For example, one cannot determine with any reasonable degree of accuracy any of the following:

- the number of new general-purpose computers installed during any particular year;
- the amount and kind of software produced and in existence;
- the number of programmers and the growth rate of the programmer population;
- the productivity of those programmers and the rate of change of this productivity over time.

The last of the above items is of utmost concern. Without these base-line supply and demand values, how is one to evaluate any of the proposed solutions to "the software problem"? With respect to the last item, there is no available data on how much software is presently (or ever has been) maintained, nor do we have any idea of what the growth rate of this "inventory" of software is, nor of this inventory's distribution in terms of size and kind. Equally unknown is the amount of software that is discarded from the inventory or that never becomes part of the inventory. We also do not know how much software is produced in support of developing an application or a system. If we are ever to properly measure the productivity of programmers, we must know how much undeliverable or non-installable software is created for the various kinds of software that *is* delivered and installed.

2. IN THE BEGINNING

When computers first became available as usable tools more than twenty years ago, practically all of the programs that were written for them were application programs. The early computers were function-ally slow, small, and simple. The IBM 701, for example, which was introduced in the early 1950's, had only 32 instructions and the manual for it was 103 pages long [IBM 1953]. The programs that were written for these computers were also relatively small and simple, limited not only by the constraints of the computer but also by the simple and crude tools available for program creation and "debugging." Programs were tested against hand-generated test cases, which often were laboriously prepared. Each program was "maintained" by the programmer who wrote it. Each program that was written was relatively unique, in that the programmer was attempting to do something that had not been done before. It was either a new application, or the implementation of a new technique, or a major improvement over earlier attempts. Combined into the single effort, then, was the "breadboard" (prototype) and the production model. Few attempts were made to redo a program for production or maintenance unless its inefficiencies were glaring. Rarely, if ever, was a program turned over to a non-programmer to use by himself. Thus, there was almost always an expert human intermediary between the end user and the computer. However, although the computers and programs were relatively simple, the operating procedures were usually voluminous and complex.

What programmers did was (and, for the most part, still is) a mystery to anyone not directly involved in the field, and the entire field (consisting, in the early 1950's, of at most a few dozen computers and a few hundred programmers) was classed as esoterica. The first problems upon which the power of the computer was brought to bear were insoluble in any other reasonable way; data processing was not applied to replacing existing methods. The value of the solution to the user was generally so great that the cost of programming was of little, if any, concern. And although programming was a labor-intensive activity, its economics were opposite from today's—people were *relatively* inexpensive, while computing power was *relatively* very expensive. The small numbers of both computers and programmers, and the projections of little, if any, growth in the data processing field made the (then unrecognized) problem of programmer productivity of little concern to anyone.

One of the major preoccupations of early programmers was the efficiency of their programs in terms of the minimum number of instructions or machine cycles executed to perform a given function. The trade-off between space (memory) and time was well understood. The introduction, in 1956, of FORTRAN was met with derision by many experienced programmers because of the somewhat lower efficiency of the FORTRAN-generated code relative to what a "crack" programmer could produce, and because every programmer believed that he or she was one of the best. In fact, many assembly language programs were less efficient than similar programs generated by FORTRAN. This was an early example of a more general principle that can be best stated as follows:

If a programming tool can be used in ways that frequently lead to inefficiency, it is a poor tool.

The crudity of the available tools and the continual duplication of effort (e.g., the rewritting of programs to compute standard mathematical functions) soon became obvious. Although no centrally-directed effort was mounted to solve the problem, improved tools—such as symbolic assemblers, trace routines, conventions for subroutine linkages, and subroutine libraries—began to evolve. Thus were born the system programmers; they were the programmers who preferred the tool-building-and-tending functions. They provided the tools (i.e., system programs) that, in turn, served the programmers whom we have defined in Chapter 3 as the mid users.

The creation of program libraries made the problems of testing and documentation more complex. Since a library program was written to be used by many other programmers, it had to be explained directly and simply, yet completely, covering such topics as the amount of memory and the amount of "scratch" storage it required, and special conventions, algorithms, and testing procedures it used. But since the data processing communities were generally small and geographically local, communication among providers and users was easy and direct, often extending beyond company boundaries. A library submission implied that the creator of the program would also be the maintainer; errors discovered by others were the creator's to fix. New variations created by another programmer were that programmer's responsibility.

As the benefits of sharing commonly useful programs at the local level became more obvious, the equally obvious solution on a nation-wide basis was the inception of user groups, beginning with SHARE in 1955. These user groups served their respective communities in many ways: as mechanisms for centralized collection and distribution of generally useful programs, as vehicles for creating standards pertinent to those programs, and as centralized collective voices through which to deal with vendors in the common interests of users, particularly concerning hardware-related issues, but eventually extending into issues regarding vendor-supplied software.

3. TWENTY YEARS LATER

Evolution of the data processing industry has continued (with some minor revolutions), and change is strongly evident; but whether there has been any real and lasting progress in the software development area is an open issue. Twenty years later, there are still two readily distinguishable types of programmers: system programmers and applications programmers. Within the latter class there are two obvious subdivisions that have always seemed to exist: scientific (or engineering) and business (or commercial). Taxonomy aside, the point is that all programmers are no longer brothers; they are divided into tribes and clans that do not necessarily have totally common interests or similar definitions of the general welfare. What they do have in common is that they all produce software.

Today's computers are generally more complex and are constructed from highly sophisticated components. The IBM System/370 (any model) has well in excess of 100 instructions and an architecture that a Rip Van Winkle of the IBM 701 era would have difficulty recognizing, and requires thousands of pages to describe. Today, a general-purpose computer is rarely delivered as a raw piece of hardware, as was an IBM 701 or any other computer of that era; it comes with a great deal of complex software, the main components of which are a system control program (operating system), language processors (not all of which are free), and a large grab bag of data access methods, data-base and data management tools, and other sundry utility programs. The necessary "documentation" that describes the things an applications programmer must understand in order to be able to do his or her job fills a very large bookshelf. The programs that applications programmers are asked to write are relatively complex, but their tools for *creating* them are considerably more powerful. On the other hand, "debugging" and testing aids have *not* improved to anywhere near the same level of power and sophistication. Test cases are still laboriously prepared by hand, and memory dumps are in absolute octal or hexadecimal.

Other things also have not changed. A large number of programs are still unique, because they represent attempts to do something never done before, but far too frequently new programs are written because of the attitude that software "not invented here" is, ipso facto, suspect. Worse, the industry still tends to build prototypes, but now they get delivered into the hands of the end users with little or no thought given to these users' ability to cope with the technological intricacies of what has been built. There is often no expert intermediary between the user and the data processing system; admittedly, the operating procedures have been somewhat simplified and standardized by incorporating them in the "job control language" of the system control program, thus eliminating the voluminous and complex manual procedures of the past.

The economics of data processing have changed drastically. The ratio of hardware to software costs in the 1950's was about 4 to 1; today it is close to 1 to 4 [Boehm 1973]. Data processing systems are pervasive, and the increasing number of programmers required to produce and maintain software has become a major concern [Bylinsky 1967]. The high-payoff, low-risk applications are rare, and the cost of high-payoff, high-risk applications is a questionable investment. Productivity of programmers has increased by no more than a factor of four (as measured in number of instructions installed per man-year), while the cost per man-hour has grown as fast or faster.

Although we speak freely (and often glibly) of "computer science," "information science," and "software and programming technology," programming has *not* evolved beyond being a craft.[1] It is not based on any science; the only universal law that has been proposed is that of Böhm and Jacopini [1966], which holds that any program can be constructed from three basic units, and which forms the basis for structured programming. There exists no *theory* of computer algorithms [Knuth 1973] or of programming; but because programming deals with techniques that are related to mathematics and to the various sciences, and because everything that is to be implemented must be quantified, one often tends to hold rather strongly the belief that one is engaged in science and technology where the creation and production of programs (software) is concerned. Yet there is not one shred of evidence to support this belief today; it is held simply as an article of faith. Programming remains a craft that many people can learn regardless of background, education, experience, etc., but that most never learn well.

Not only is programming a craft, it is probably the most complex craft ever invented. One of the major reasons for this complexity has been well stated by Dijkstra [1974]:

When dealing with "mastered complexity," the idea of a hierarchy seems to be a key concept. The notion of a hierarchy implies that

---

1. A craft industry is one in which things are done the way they have been done before, rather than as some theory would indicate [Jones 1970]. If any "theory" at all can be said to exist, it is a theory of practice, not one of content or substance.

what at one level is regarded as an unanalyzed unit, is regarded as a composite object at the next lower level of greater detail, for which the appropriate grain (say, of time or space) is an order of magnitude smaller than the corresponding grain appropriate at the next higher level. As a result, the number of levels that can meaningfully be distinguished in a hierarchical composition is approximately proportional to the logarithm of the ratio between the largest and the smallest grain. In programming, where the total computation may take an hour, while the smallest time grain is in the order of a microsecond, we have an environment in which this ratio can easily exceed 10^9 and I know of no other environment in which a single technology has to encompass so wide a span.

Furthermore, software is not bound by any natural laws in its manipulation of data. In that sense, it is analogous to the animated motion picture. The objects in an animated film may behave in any way that the animator desires, being limited only by his imagination and the physical limitations of the medium. The same is true of a program. The programmer may cause practically any arbitrary sequence of logical and arithmetic manipulations he desires to be performed on the data; and so long as the results remain within the range of values acceptable to the hardware, all else is permitted. He can create negative time or a retrograde moon for the earth, accelerate a particle well beyond the speed of light, or compute a paycheck for a nonexistent employee. Until and unless some human agent discovers these "violations," there are no complaints from anyone or anything, and certainly not from the computer.

The fact that programming is a craft does not imply that it has no intellectual content. Programming encompasses many separable activities, the most important of which is that of organizing and structuring a problem solution (the algorithm) and related data for automatic execution by a data processing system. In many instances, it is also left to the programmer to discover that solution or algorithm. Also included in programming (as the task is most often thought of) is the actual implementation (often referred to as "coding") of the solution in a computer-processable language, and the subsequent steps of removing the flaws and errors, both logical and mechanical, called "debugging" and testing. Then follows integration, installation, and maintenance. *Maintenance* is concerned with two distinct aspects of software: one is the correction of remaining flaws and errors; the other is the modification and improvement that result from changes in the environment and from the user's desires, requests, and demands, or from the programmer's perception and anticipation of them.[2]

Programming, then, is not a mechanical or rote activity or one of the simple application of skills, but requires rather high intellectual competence. For example, for the purposes of determining whether or not certain programmers are to be considered "exempt" (from the overtime and other provisions of the Fair Labor Standards Act), the U.S. Department of Labor specifies that several tests be applied. One such test attempts to determine whether or not at least half of the work performed by a computer programmer is of "substantial importance to the conduct of business," and gives an example of what "substantial importance" means: "assists in the design and development of computer programs," while "codes and debugs programs" is considered "not of substantial importance." A second and equally important test is whether or not the programmer "customarily and regularly exercises discretion and independent judgment as distinguished from using skills." Thus, according to the U.S. Department of Labor, one who applies knowledge in following prescribed procedures or determining which procedure to follow, or who determines whether specified standards are met is not exercising discretion and independent judgment. In this instance, the Department of Labor guidance reads, in part, "Every problem processed in a computer first must be carefully analyzed so that exact and logical steps for its solution can be worked out. When this work is done by a computer programmer, he is exercising discretion and independent judgment." One could substantively argue with the Department of Labor guidance that implies that coding and "debugging" are "not of substantial importance to the conduct of business," but that is not the point. It is that programming is not a simple exercise in the application of a set of skills and procedures, but requires discretion and judgment at all levels of performance; and if, in fact, it is not a "professional" activity, it is one with considerable intellectual content.

The fact that software is the product of a craft lies at the heart of most of the problems facing the data processing industry today. Each craftsman organizes and codes his program in his own individual way, there being no other practical alternative, although the proponents of structured programming claim otherwise. Although there are conventions to be followed, and other constraints are imposed, the remaining freedom and lack of standards and measures militate against efforts

---

2. This definition of the term "maintenance" is unique to the programming craft.

to exert sufficient control over the process. This reliance on craftsman-
ship (the *average* level of which is, in any case, relatively low for many
reasons) will limit the economic growth and expansion of the industry
unless the necessary and appropriate steps are taken to remedy the
situation.

Viewing the present situation from another perspective, at the
center of the data processing environment is the computer itself (over
whose architecture the user exerts at best indirect influence). The system control program aids the user in manipulating and managing the
computer's resources and logically expanding its functional capability,
and users can exert some direct influence on that basic software but
cannot completely control its structure and function. Users also have
the sundry supporting software, such as language processors, "debugging" tools, and utility programs, over which they now have substantial
influence, either as designers or as implementors; but, with the passage
of time, the users will exert less and less control, as even these supporting items fall more and more within the purview and control of the
vendor.

On top of the system control program and other supporting software
reside the application programs that perform the processing that makes
the totality of the data processing system necessary or desirable to the
end user. These applications may be programmed by the end user
himself, by specialists dedicated to his or her application area, or by
journeymen programmers from various sources. It is toward improving
the effectiveness of these people in terms of productivity, reliability of
their work products, and the general perceived quality of the end result
of their work that the data processing industry's efforts must be
directed. This is the topic to which the remainder of this chapter is
devoted.

4. A PERCEPTION OF THE PROBLEM

4.1. The System Control Program Interface

In the early days of computing, practically every programmer was an
applications programmer. His principal interface was with the raw
hardware, and his support was a simple language processor and a small
library of utility routines. That is rarely so today. The principal interface for the applications programmer *today* is the system control
program (SCP), which is far more complex than the hardware. This

interface, in its intricacy and in the abundance of opportunities it offers for misunderstandings and mistakes, is the object of many complaints. The complexity of the SCP—which is due, in part, to its having absorbed the functions of resource management, data management, and data access, among other things—results not only in greater power for its users but also in great difficulty in understanding its full capability and the full impact of each user's actions. The designer's goal for an SCP should be to create one that is readily understandable by the average applications programmer but that still retains its full capability. Learning and effectively using the "job control languages" of present SCPs is a major undertaking, while cataloged procedures tend to institutionalize some forms of superstition by making it easier to use what is known to work rather than to determine what would work best (or even just better). The only reason why programs can be written that perform as expected is that the hardware is reliable and obedient—reliable, that is, in the sense that its continuous strict obedience to the programmed instructions can be relied on. Although SCPs have now become an inherent part of the programming environment, they are unfortunately not as reliable and obedient as the hardware. With each release, version, or temporary fix, users' reliance on an SCP's strict obedience is shaken.

Stability of an SCP over long periods of time is a most desirable goal. While the programmer's interface with the *hardware* has been generally stable for some time (owing primarily to compatible hardware families, e.g., IBM System/360 and System/370 series, UNIVAC 1100 series, etc.), SCPs have been continually changing, necessitating accompanying changes in the application programs that are dependent upon them. In the best of all possible worlds, an SCP should appear to its users as a uniform, logical, and stable extension of the functions embodied in the hardware. (The characteristics of an Installation Control Program—ICP—and the division of labor between an SCP and an ICP have been discussed in Section 4 of Chapter 3.)

The movement toward, as well as the general acceptance of database oriented systems *should* permit simplification of the external interfaces of both the SCPs and the ICPs, so that the mid user's interfaces with a data processing system could again be as consistent as they were with the early operating systems, when an average of four control statements was needed to run most jobs (often, however, requiring voluminous written operating procedures); but the utter simplicity of "the good old days" will never return.

It is quite possible that the typical SCP of 1985 will be embedded in the hardware (just like the IBM 370/145's microcoded instruction control program) and that the storage used for its execution will be fenced off from access by the user. This idea is not new, but its proper implementation will require considerable rethinking of the conceptual basis for an SCP. Above all, reliability, stability, and longevity of SCPs are most desirable, but only if these SCPs truly meet the users' needs.

Given the necessary pressure, support, and cooperation from both vendors and users, by 1985 the SCP is likely to become as inviolate as today's hardware and will provide the necessary standard interfaces for the ICP and other software.

4.2. Resource Management and Availability

Although the programmer or the end user specifies the resources (including not only the processing resources but the data as well) required to run the software that performs the functions required by an application, the end user has no control, beyond making the initial request, over the actual execution of the specified procedures. A combination of the human machine operator and the SCP actually controls the resources of the system. All that the user may do is *request* the necessary resources for the job. Actual resource allocation is generally beyond his control and usually resides in another arm of his organization, or even totally outside his company. Only when the end user is on-line to an interactive system does he have direct contact with some portion of the operational entity. Thus, planning for the resource needs has a direct impact on the quality of service delivered to both the applications software developer and to the ultimate end user of that software. Rarely is an installation willing and able to maintain a supply of computing resources beyond the immediate need.

Another aspect of the problem is that, unlike some commodities (pencils and tablets, for example), the minimum increment of capacity that can be acquired for a general-purpose data processing system is quite large (and usually quite expensive in several ways). For instance, today, on the larger IBM systems, main memory can be increased only by million-byte increments; and if one needs more than two million bytes and has an IBM 370/145, one has to step up to an IBM 370/158. Although the situation is not necessarily quite so severe in all instances (adding two more disk spindles when one already has thirty is but a small increase), it is generally a serious problem for the average installation. In other words, capacity cannot be made to grow in a close approximation to a continuous function, but rather must follow a step function with uncomfortably large dollar steps[3] and time delays. Peak load periods create conflicts that must be resolved by negotiation or by other, less desirable, methods. The problem is further compounded because it is difficult to know when the resource is running low; there is no "gas" gauge.

Indeed, there are two facets to the problem of spare (or excess) capacity: one concerns the system upon which the end users depend to get their work done; the other concerns the system upon which new applications are developed. Each creates its own demand for spare capacity. When these two systems are embodied in a single computer, the problems of managing that resource are multiplied.

These problems are exacerbated because our industry is in a continuously evolving world, and last year's experience must be discounted heavily when applying it to next year's problems. The fact that the industry is moving into an era that is heavily centered around data bases implies that the hierarchy of storage systems that are understood today will change to reflect, even more strongly, the way one deals with data. There will be a continuous movement of data up and down the levels of this hierarchy, from relatively slow trillion-bit (or larger) stores to relatively small, nanosecond "cache" stores. Determining the proper mix of such stores for a given installation and measuring the resulting system's performance will be a complex problem, since there will be major conflicts between the extremes of the requirements of the various application programs in the installation.

By 1985, many (but by no means all) of today's problems associated with automatic resource management and scheduling will have been solved.

4.3. Cost of Producing Software

One of the industry's most visible problems, and one that is at the top of almost everyone's list, is the cost of producing software of all kinds. That cost must be measured not only in dollars per instruction, but in elapsed time, duplication of effort, resources expended, and the indirect costs of delayed installation of a system. This is another symptom of the fact that programming is a craft. Although the situation may be improving somewhat, estimating and controlling the cost of software production is still primarily guesswork. Usually, it is based on an

---

3. We propose a possible partial solution to this problem in Section 5.5 of Chapter 7.

estimate of the number of lines of code for each of a number of modules of estimated complexity, with these estimates strongly influenced by the (not well understood) design of the program and by its external constraints. A *lack of understanding* of the proper relationship between requirements and the various steps needed to implement a program that meets these requirements, as well as of the applicable trade-offs and penalties, is a severe deficiency. Unless and until the industry can learn to control the total process, from conception to installation and use, it cannot gain control over costs, to say nothing of alleviating the mismatch between needs and requirements on the one hand, and actual implementation on the other.

As new techniques have come into the programming world, they have been touted to contain the necessary ingredients to solve the cost (productivity) problem, sometimes to the the point that they have become fads. Higher-level languages were the first purported solution. There is no denying that they have been helpful, but it is not true that if a little bit helps, a lot more will be much better. There is no longer any reason to believe that a newer, better, general-purpose programming language will make a measurable difference in programmer productivity. This is not to say that all further language development should stop, but just that it should be understood that there is no magic in new programming languages, that the best we can expect are small, incremental gains, and that, as such, new languages are acceptable (and sometimes even welcome), provided that their cost is not excessive.

The disenchantment with new languages—when it finally did occur—did not shake the industry's deep belief in magic: many of the same purported improvements of the programming process that were previously attributed to new languages were then simply re-attributed to interactive (time-sharing) systems. Many still believe those unsupportable claims. Again, this is not to say that interactive systems do not materially help to increase productivity of some facets of software development, but rather that they are not a panacea.

Currently, the industry seems to be repeating this process in regard to structured programming and its derivatives. The proponents of structured programming claim enormous improvements in cost and quality, and its detractors claim that it is not universally applicable and that there is not (and may never be) sufficient data upon which to make a proper judgment. The truth probably lies somewhere between these two extreme positions.

It is indicative of the general immaturity of the data processing industry that a new technique is either praised to the sky with unsupportable claims or condemned out of hand. The claims or condemnations are not in themselves immature, but there are no base-line data against which to make a properly controlled evaluation and trade-off analysis. For example, the concept of programmer productivity is at best ill defined. It is not clear that machine instructions produced per man-month is a reasonable measure or the one that will suffice to determine whether a proposed change in methodology will have the desired effect on productivity and other related costs.

If, by 1985, the issues of measures, productivity, value, and quality as they relate to software and its development are not resolved, we cannot expect to see, let alone know whether we are making, improvements. Although there is an intuitive feeling that the data processing industry's growth will be limited by the inability to produce the necessary software unless there is nearly an order-of-magnitude improvement in productivity, there exists no way to either substantiate or refute that feeling today. Ten or so years from now, if nothing more than intuition is available to guide the industry's choices, the growth of the industry will be stunted. One very valuable by-product of being able to measure and evaluate various aspects of the software development process will be that, although it will probably remain a craft for some time, it will become a better understood craft.

4.4. Control of Software Production

There can be no control of software production unless the managers and programmers understand the programming process well enough so that the necessary discipline and accountability can be installed in the production environment. By accountability we mean that, in every program produced, one can identify the programmer who wrote each line and that when an error occurs or a fault is detected, the programmer whose code was the source of the problem is readily known, so that he is therefore accountable. To date, the industry has not acquired a sufficient level of understanding and discipline to do this, but there are efforts, studies, suggestions, and projects underway that potentially could lead to that end. There are, however, implications that one should be aware of. The individual programmers will lose some of the "freedom" they now enjoy, and accountability will force the marginal craftsmen out of the ranks. On the other hand, since there will always be (by definition) a shortage of superior people, most programs will be written by average people, and any system of assignment and accountability must take this fact into account. Greater problems will occur in trying to extend accountability to the part-time ("moonlighting") programmer. For certain critical programs, the need for accountability may limit the manner in which they may be produced. Accountability cannot, however, remove the necessity for each programmer to produce software that is readily understandable and maintainable by another programmer, and that is generally transferable from one programmer to another at any point in the process of development and maintenance.

By 1985, accountability of programmers for their respective product will be an accepted concept. Means for transferring responsibility and accountability from one programmer or group of programmers to another will be well understood and in common use.

4.5. Trade-offs in Software Design

No complex product designed by man is perfect. Unlike software, however, most manufactured products undergo some trade-off analyses in efforts to arrive at the best engineering compromise where conflicts arise between cost and function, or between manufacturing cost and complexity, on the one hand, and maintenance, repairability, etc., on the other. Unfortunately, such trade-off studies are rarely performed for software development projects. One primary reason, of course, is that there is little or no data on the basis of which to perform such studies. Although most programmers understand, at least intuitively, the trade-off between storage space and execution time, even that trade-off is one over which, today, they do not often have—or are not permitted to exercise—control; but the areas for which they are, at best, minimally prepared are those involving the economics of the data processing milieu. For example, although it may actually save several man-days to design and implement a facet of an interactive system so that it requires a user to respond with two keystrokes rather than one, the cost to the end user in added effort, irritation, and reduced productivity may greatly outweigh the original saving. Studies of such trade-offs, if they are done, are rarely published. Among the things that are of material importance if the craft of developing software is to be improved are the ability to get definitive answers to questions (which are illustrative rather than definitive) such as:

- Is there an economic justification for "locking" an SCP?
- For a complex system, is it better to simulate it, or to construct a breadboard?

- Which implementation language or technique minimizes the cost of subsequent change and maintenance?
- What are the cost implications to the implementors, maintainers, and users of a given data base structure?
- How much (quantitatively) will a particular new language or programming methodology improve the average programmer's productivity?

Most people in the industry have intuitive answers to these questions and to many more like them, but they would be hard pressed to quantitatively back up their intuitions with data, statistics, and sound dollar-and-cents figures. Unless and until they can, essentially all major improvements to the software development craft will be accidental.

Given proper emphasis and impetus, much of the data and understanding required to perform meaningful trade-off analyses will be available by 1985. Unfortunately, the resulting impact will not be felt until the following decade.

4.6. Robustness

There is an aspect of software that is difficult to define, impossible to measure, conceded to be desirable, but outside of today's state of the art. It is best connoted by the word "robust." Almost everyone has some concept of the robustness of software, but it has yet to be rigorously defined. It means, in part, that an entire system should not fall apart just because a single bit in some line of code fails. It means that the software should be designed with error containment as a primary goal, should be fault-tolerant, and should be forgiving of user mistakes. In a slightly different dimension, it means that software must be designed to be robust enough to undergo the continually evolving changes to which it is subjected; in other words, it must be robust not only for those who use it, but also for those who modify it. It appears to be a qualitative property, rather than a quantitative one, but a mandatory one for the future. It has been estimated that 30% of the U.S. labor force presently depends on data processing to accomplish its work. By 1980, that fraction will increase to 50% and, by 1985, to 70% [Boehm 1973], if we can accommodate the growth. That the software upon which the majority of the U.S. labor force depends must be robust is a foregone conclusion, but how to make it so is an outstanding problem.

Before robustness can become a general property of software, much basic work is still needed in analyzing failure modes, recovery methods, techniques for detecting and containing errors, and in several other areas. On the other hand, we expect that, in certain critical or unique cases, there will be examples of robust software by 1985.

4.7. Performance Cost of Using Software

Another important aspect of software is related to the problem of operational management and control; it is the cost of using (or misusing) software. Although the concept of efficient object programs was a dominant one in the early days, when the computing resource was scarce, it has been conspicuous by its absence in recent times. When applications software is conceived and designed, rarely are the operational costs taken into account—not just the central processor cycles required and the number of cylinders or packs needed for the data, but all of the attendant costs, such as the cost of preparing the input, the "job setup" cost, and the costs of initiating and running the job, interpreting the output, and getting the results to the end user. This is one very important trade-off study we do not yet know how to do properly. Stating it another way (and repeating the principle put forth earlier), if a program can frequently be used in ways that are generally inefficient, then it is a poor program. The problem obviously encompasses more than just software: it involves the total methodology, systems, and personnel needed to get a job done. In addition, there are learning and training costs, the cost of mistakes and errors at any and every step, as well as the cost of the software (or of the system) that is *not* being used, or is being subverted by the people for whom it was intended but who were not involved in the design or decision to implement and install, and thus to whom the system is unacceptable. The point is that *software cannot be viewed in isolation;* it is part of a larger scheme, even though designers and implementors of software habitually tend to ignore everything that is not in their immediate purview. In a sense, the applications developers are as guilty as the system programmers who are accused of ignoring the applications developers. The problems associated with performance costs will begin to yield to solution only when many of the problems spoken of above begin to be faced squarely, and when the broad view becomes the prevalent one.

4.8. User-Perceived Quality

All of the above aspects of data processing systems can be combined to cover the attribute that we call "user-perceived quality." This term focuses particular attention on concepts derived from the field called ergonomics or human engineering. Concepts such as ease of use, minimization of inadvertent errors, "fail soft," recovery, forgiveness, etc., must become an integral part of the conception and design of all software. Included is an understanding by designers and developers of the end users' perception of the way things should be done and of what impact or considerations must be attributed to these perceptions in a proper trade-off study.[4] Although such considerations may raise the cost of installed applications, we believe that the eventual savings in both hidden and overt costs will more than make up for this increase. The balance between near-term savings and long-term cost of use is another trade-off element that is not well understood and is therefore paid little more than lip service.

Only continued and concentrated pressure on the part of the users and those who pay for software will bring this problem to its proper level of appreciation. That pressure is beginning to emerge and, if sustained, will force major improvements (with attendant increased costs) in delivered software by 1985.

We also observe that, in the data processing industry (unlike most other industries), improvements in quality tend to improve productivity, and vice versa. This unique characteristic of the data processing craft should be consciously exploited.

4.9. Productivity of Applications Development

Applications development productivity is evaluated according to the following criteria:

- total cost to develop the system;
- amount and kind of resources consumed in the development process;
- elapsed time to completion;
- complexity of the implementation process and of the resultant system;
- amount and kind of resources consumed by the production use of the resultant system;
- quality of the resultant system:
  - as perceived by the end users (see Section 4.8 of this chapter);
  - as perceived by its maintainers.

---

4. We have discussed the users' point of view on this topic in Section 1.2 of Chapter 3.

Some of the factors that affect productivity are:

- energy and skill of individual workers;
- suitability of available tools;
- efficiency of the team structure;
- wisdom of market analysis and product objectives;
- breadth of distribution of the end product.

The industry's past and present experience shows clearly that, as the size, complexity, and demand for reliability of the applications systems being developed increase, the development productivity, as described above, worsens very rapidly [Poupard et al. 1973; Kosy 1974; Brooks 1975]. Our projection of the types of systems that will be implemented around 1985 indicates very substantial increases in their size and complexity. It is easy to identify systems that are so large and complex that elapsed time for implementation, utilizing today's development techniques, could well exceed the expected stable life of the system or of the organization that needs the system in the first place [Kosy 1974]. The message is clear: significant progress must be made in applications development productivity if the large, complex applications envisioned today are to be practical (i.e., implementable) tomorrow.

The problem, here, is assessing the potential solutions for improvement of applications development productivity. Improvements in procedure-oriented languages[5] such as PL/I, COBOL, and FORTRAN do not have the potential for improving productivity by as much as a factor of two, while an improvement of at least one decimal order of magnitude is a necessity, and more would be desirable.

A quick look at today's data processing applications reveals a shocking amount of redundant effort throughout the data processing community. As an example, the collective number of man-years devoted, over the last ten years, by the "Fortune 500" companies to the development and maintenance of personnel records and payroll systems is, we suspect, unconscionable; we also suspect that it might be disheartening—but instructive—to learn the number of man-years still being spent each year by these companies on the development and maintenance of such systems. And yet, this is a fairly well-defined application area; there are only a limited number of legitimate variations in requirements.

---

5. We do mean to distinguish here between *programming* languages and *"requirement specification"* languages. The latter are badly needed, as we point out below.

A substantial number of additional applications areas have similar characteristics. Looking below the applications level, the number of modules of code or parts of programs that perform identical (or nearly identical) functions is staggering. (One large company today has, in *one* data processing center, *seventeen* COBOL routines for computing, from a given date, the number of days-in-year to that date.)

Many attempts have been made to market "generalized" applications systems, aimed either at a given industry or at the general business market. These systems have usually met with limited acceptance for a variety of reasons, e.g.:

- Capabilities of a "generalized" application system are so limited that they require significant modifications of the user requirements to fit that system.
- Attempts at generality have caused relatively inefficient use of hardware resources, as compared to tailored systems.
- Potential users are concerned about the capability of the vendor to provide responsive, long-term maintenance.

Yet, in contrast to the lack of acceptance of such "generalized" applications systems, there is a rapidly growing tendency to obtain general, applications-oriented *tools* from various vendors. Mathematical programming systems, statistical packages, report generators, file management systems, and data management and data-base systems are popular examples.

A new, well-accepted, and somewhat promising approach came on the scene with the advent of the IBM System/3. The parameterized applications generator is an approach with substantial potential, although the System/3 packages are, at best, a modest beginning.

In short, the industry is beginning to get away from the "my square root routine is better than your square root routine" syndrome, although it still has a long way to go.

Some general characteristics of the solutions to the problem of applications development productivity can be identified:

- The solutions must minimize the percentage of total software in a new application that is *new* software. Today, perhaps 80% to 90% of the software required for a new application is newly developed (excluding the SCP). This is the basic reason for cost, elapsed development time, and quality problems. This percentage should be reduced to 10% to 20%.

- The solutions must reduce the rate at which the results of programming efforts are rendered obsolete. At present, relatively minor changes in requirements, business procedures, policies, etc., often obsolete many man-years of programming effort. The industry must learn how to measure and maximize the "half-life" of a line of installed code.

- The solutions must broaden the usefulness of the new software that is generated. When new software does have to be generated, it should be designed in such a way that it can be reused whenever identical or similar functions are required in other development efforts.

- The solutions must significantly reduce the present requirements for specialized skills, experience, and training needed in order for one to qualify as an applications developer, so that, eventually, the end user himself can become that developer.

- The solutions must significantly raise the acceptable minimum levels of productivity of individual software developers and of the quality of the resultant applications.

- The solutions must materially aid in overcoming the communication problems associated with the definition of applications requirements. At present, there exist major discrepancies between what the end user *said,* what the analyst or system implementor *heard,* and what the resulting application actually *does.*

- The solutions must eliminate, or at least drastically reduce, the variability in the structural design of an application that is introduced by different designers and implementors. In today's environment, the identical system specification given to different system designers results in as many different designs as there are designers, and the same is true for different implementors and their respective implementations.

If this set of requirements can be met, an order-of-magnitude improvement in productivity would be a near certainty, and a larger improvement might well be possible. But it is not at all clear that it will happen by 1985.

4.10. Some Unexplored Properties of Software

There are those who are firmly convinced that, left unattended, software "rots." Conceptually, that seems to be impossible, for, unlike organic material, software appears to contain no active agent that could induce a spontaneous change in its constitution. It may be that a software module itself undergoes no change, but that the minimal and usually insufficient documentation and explanation of its intent, purpose, usage, conventions, and restrictions do, over time, degrade to a point at which the software itself appears to have "rotted." Changes in the environment—both subtle and obvious—can also induce the appearance of software rot. Additions or changes to the hardware configuration can cause software that has been well behaved for long periods of time to degrade surprisingly quickly. Although this kind of degradation is more difficult to prevent a priori, it should be anticipated and accommodated as part of the change. This form of software rot can be prevented, and, as is so true in many other circumstances, the cost of prevention is usually considerably less than the cost of a cure.

One other phenomenon that is readily observable is that the software that is most heavily used and depended upon is continually changed. It is changed for many reasons—to repair faults, to make it more efficient, to adapt it to a newly-acquired function, to improve it, etc. Given that one can "account" for every "instruction"[6] in a newly released module or software system, can one determine the "half-life" of an instruction over the life-cycle of that software? Is the half-life of an instruction in some kinds of software longer than in others? Is the half-life of an instruction in a compiler longer or shorter than that of an instruction in an operating system, or in a mathematical subroutine, or a payroll package? If such a measure[7] were available, the life-cycle costs of installing, using, and maintaining software could be estimated more relevantly and accurately, and some attempt could be made to solve the problems associated with maximizing the half-life of particular classes of software, if not of all software in general. Today, no such measure is available, nor are the data from which to derive such a measure being collected.

4.11. Summary of the Problem

The process of software development must be made manageable. The programming craft must be better understood, and individual accountability, quality assurance, and other necessary measures must be

---

6. The word "instruction" is used here in its most general sense, e.g., a line of FORTRAN code, a JCL statement, a macro call.

7. The half-life of an instruction is used here as an example. We are not necessarily suggesting that this particular measure is the correct one.

instituted. The craft products themselves, subject to all of the bounding and constraining conditions discussed above, must become useful, robust, high-quality software that will attract end users, rather than repel them. Under management pressure, the craft may mature into a controllable, accountable, understood, and quantifiable process, but whether software development will ever become a technology is an open question. Under any circumstance, management pressure, economic and social pressure, and dedicated research and development efforts will be required to change the condition of the software development craft in a meaningful way by 1985.

5. SUPPORTING TOOLS FOR APPLICATIONS

5.1. Standard Structures

Were it possible to devise a standard basic structure that is common to many applications, much time and effort could be conserved. One method that has been suggested (and that is being explored in various places) is the creation of a simulation system (which, in itself, would automatically bring some structure to the problem) in which it would be possible to specify the design for a program or system without generating all of the new modules of code required [Bachman and Bouvard 1972]. This would permit evaluation of the design of the program by its users before a total commitment of the implementation resources is made. Properly done, the simulation would permit validation by the user (and the implementation of changes to suit the user's needs) long before the program was turned over to him. The user then would become an involved, integral member of the design effort and would know what product he can eventually expect. Further, the simulation system should permit organized replacement of each simulated module with the real thing, thus eventually achieving a complete transition from a simulated program to an actual one. A further benefit may accrue from such an approach: if a collection of simulated standard structures were built, the temptation to reinvent (as well as the justification for reinventing) the existing elements might be minimized.

5.2. Building Blocks

The concept of the module or building block must be extended beyond reusable software modules to incorporate essentially all of the software that is being produced. This modularity should be inherent in the way programs are created. For this to happen, the concept of building blocks with standard documentation and with standard interfaces and communication among them must be better defined than it is at present. The problem is not impossibly large; the solution consists in encouraging the proper attitude and in imposing the necessary discipline.

One aspect of the solution that is not easily achieved, but that is a necessity for truly transferable, general-purpose building blocks, is a form of data independence. This is not to say that building blocks should not be data driven, but that the form or format of the data transmitted to the building block should not matter, so long as the required range and precision of the given representations are met. This would reduce the amount of effort required to produce a new application that is a variant or an extension of an existing one.

Enlarging the concept further, complete independence of a module or a program from the data is most desirable. It implies that an algorithm or process that is generally applicable to a wide variety of data need be written only once. Some data-independent programs and modules already exist, and the generalization of this concept has deep implications for the structure of both systems and data bases.

5.3. Data-Base Oriented Systems

There is a trend in the industry toward data-base and data-management oriented systems. There are interesting (and possibly profound) implications for application programs and applications programmers in this trend. It is reasonable to assume that more and more application programs will interface with large, common data bases. Properly organized and managed, such data bases could indeed make the applications programmer's job easier, for he would be relieved of the concerns of acquiring, organizing, managing, and accessing the data. Further, in a properly designed system, there should be little if any need for those functions of the JCL that are now the bane of many programmers: creating, opening, closing, sharing, and disposing of files or "data sets." Many applications, which in the past would have been of marginal value because of the data costs, may soon become economically attractive. This will increase the demand for new application programs and will thus increase the load on the programming staff.

There are still unsolved problems which result from looking at the world of data processing as if it were one giant collection of data bases. One of these problems is the organization and management of large data collections distributed geographically and over many hierarchical levels of storage; another is the impact on resource management resulting from the cost, usefulness, and quality of applications run on such systems. One other problem should be mentioned, that of the data being "down" (contrasted with the system being "down"). Present concepts of reliability, "recoverability," integrity, and accessibility will have to be modified to accommodate this new circumstance. (It should also be noted that although data-base oriented systems are presently in vogue, we do not dwell on them here for the primary reason that, in our opinion, they imply no new requirements that are not otherwise covered in this study.)

5.4. Computer Networks

Another major trend that may affect the way application programs are conceived and implemented is the potential emergence of computer networks (see Section 10 of Chapter 5). It may become necessary to distinguish between computers interfaced with communications networks on the one hand, and networks of computers on the other. Such a distinction is difficult to draw precisely, but distributed processing and resource sharing or load leveling will require networks of computers, while the accepted teleprocessing systems of today "simply" use communication networks. There seems to be a gray area between these two that poses the problem.

As a tool for applications programmers, networks of either kind can increase their access to data processing resources. One can conceive of development being done on a "remote" system that incorporates sophisticated tools for program development that would overburden the "local" system. Communication in such a system would be required between the programmer, the development site, and the local data base for testing and validation. As with data-base oriented systems, networks pose essentially no new or unique requirements that are not covered elsewhere in this study.

5.5. Applications Produced by the End User

A proper goal for the industry in general, and for software practitioners in particular, is to reach as soon as possible, for major applications areas, the date that Boehm [1973] calls the "50% Automation Level." This is the date on which 50% of the programs for a given area are implemented by the end user in an hour or less, with no more than a day's training. Determining that the goal has been reached for a particular industry or application area will not be easy. Since end users' competence, skills, knowledge, desires, motivations, etc., will cover a wide spectrum, the requirements for attaining the goal will vary markedly, as will the criteria for determining the level of achievement. As the demand for larger and more complex applications systems increases, and as the demand for programmers continues to exceed the supply, this appears to be the only way, barring some startling breakthrough, in which the growth of the data processing industry can continue to be sustained.

5.6. Other Tools

There are other tools that can be developed and used in the short run and that will improve the performance and productivity of programmers. Common interfaces between user programs and the ICP should be realizable. In many instances, providing an interactive environment for the software developers will be of great help, particularly for program creation, source-code management, and module (or "unit") testing. More thought and effort put into test procedures and the creation of the necessary supporting facilities could reduce the cost of development significantly. The pernicious practices that interactive systems seem to encourage, such as on-the-fly design and coding, are to be avoided at all costs; whatever benefits are locally gained by such practices will be forfeited many times over in future costs when software thus created must be frequently used, reused, and changed.

5.7. An Example

The primary purpose of this study is to point out those requirements of the end users that imply significant research or development efforts, rather than to attempt to present complete solutions to meet such requirements. It seems appropriate, however, to outline an example of the type of solution that could meet the rather severe set of requirements given above.

One can envision an "applications generator." This tool can be implemented in several different forms, each meant for a specific type of application (e.g., payroll), or for a class of applications. The developer and the applications generator would interact via a "menu" of alternative selections (primarily multiple choice, or true-false) on a television-like console. The generator would view each application as a hierarchically organized set of building blocks that are to be tied together in a manner dictated by the choices offered by the generator and selected by the developer.

At the beginning of the interaction, the choices offered to the developer would consist of high-level function or general intent alternatives. Further on in the development "session," the offered alternatives would be at more detailed functional levels, until input formats, output formats, data base requirements, etc., would be specified at the most detailed level. At every level, however, alternatives offered to the developer by the generator would be limited to those consistent with the higher-level selections already made earlier in the "session."

Such a generator cannot, of course, contain all conceivable functions that will (or might) be desired. This introduces the requirement for always being able to select an alternative that is "none of the above." In this case, the developer would write a new module (or a hierarchy of new modules) to fulfill the new requirements. This would be done in a highly standardized and structured manner, so that, once implemented and tested, the new functions would be automatically added to the applications generator and could then be selected by subsequent developers.

At the completion of the specification process, the generator would bind together the modules of code (which could consist of a combination of object modules, generated source modules, and interpretive modules) necessary to perform the specified functions. This could (and almost always would) be followed by an interactive checkout phase, where either automatically generated or user-specified test data would be run through the resulting applications system for verification by the developer and by the end user.

It seems quite feasible to develop such an applications generator for a specific type of application, such as inventory control. Although this could have a significant impact on an industry-wide basis, the effect on productivity in any one given installation would not be revolutionary. It is also conceivable that generators could be developed for broad sets of applications. A general-purpose generator for on-line transaction systems seems conceivable today, and the development of one such generator has been reported in the literature [Maynard 1974]. Given the expected requirements for this type of applications, such a generator's impact on development productivity could be substantial.

Assuming that such an approach is practical, it is easy to see how the objectives stated above could be realized. For example, if we look at the difficulties the end user encounters in trying to convey his requirements to the system developer, we can see that this approach would help by allowing the end user and the developer to work as a team in interacting with the generator; conceivably, it could also allow the end user to interact directly with the generator; the applications developer would then be needed only in situations where a new function is required.

One of the basic strengths of this approach is the prestructuring of the application that is gained by the existence of the generator and by the initiative the generator retains in its dialog with the developer. One of the severe weaknesses the industry currently suffers from is that the responsibility for initiative in application structuring is vested in the developer and is, therefore, unique for essentially every occurrence of each application. This has defeated most previous efforts to use standardized modules as building blocks in new applications.

It is apparent that this approach is an extreme departure from current development techniques. If it is, in fact, necessary to make such a substantial departure from current methods (and we believe that it is) in order to solve the programmer productivity problem, then we cannot overemphasize the need for extensive research and development efforts in this area.

6. TOWARD THE FUTURE

Software production is still in its infancy. That software practitioners rarely talk about their failures and learn little if anything from them is one indicator. That they tend to oversell what has the appearance of success is another. The industry can certainly continue to "let nature take its course" toward an unspecified future, but that future is not likely to be a desirable one. Not all of the problems delineated above will be solved by 1985, nor will the solutions that are achieved be in general use by that time. Therefore, priorities must be assigned to the entire set of problems, and the work on finding solutions to the more important ones must be started now. If the data processing environment of 1985 is to be generally more accommodating, influence must be exerted on the vendors to provide hardware and SCPs that match these clearly established needs.

The industry must start now to attempt to manage the software development craft as it exists today, and influence and redirect it toward the position of accepting and adopting the results of studies, research, and development. Individually and collectively, practitioners and managers must begin to attack the problems that are most pressing and to share the results of their efforts. They must appreciate the need for, as well as work toward a useful and applicable set of industry standards.

Both the producers and the users of software must accept the fact that a very large (if not the largest) part of the cost of a software system over its lifetime is due to *change,* and that methods must be developed for designing and implementating software that is well suited to this state of constant change (in requirements, in data structures, in interfaces, in underlying hardware and SCPs, etc.), thus minimizing the costs of change.

By the early 1980's, with concerted and cooperative efforts, the industry should have made major steps toward a better relationship between requirements, design, and implementation, and should also have a better understanding of the end user. The quality of the software product will have improved noticeably, but not necessarily by orders of magnitude. A sufficient number of applications areas will have reached the "50% Automation Level" to demonstrate that the goal of almost full (say, 90%) automation is achievable.

7. SUMMARY OF PROBLEMS AND RECOMMENDATIONS

Although some of the tools and techniques that are needed are already available, and although others exist in the prototype or experimental state, there are a number of problems that will require the initiation of new research projects, and others that will require a large application of common sense and good business and management practices. We list them below.

Since everything within the data processing environment affects application programs or their implementation in some way, no attempt will be made to confine the following list strictly to the applications themselves; on the other hand, no claim is made that the following is a complete delineation of all of the problems in the software area:

• The need to improve the productivity of applications programmers and of the applications development process is a very difficult and urgent problem. Every effort undertaken toward improving software should contribute to its solution. Related directly to this problem is the lack of a proper measure of programmer productivity. One must be developed. It must be kept in mind, however, that the existence of a measure does not automatically bring forth control or better management; rather, a measure is necessary for determining *whether* control and improved management are being achieved.

- New implementation languages, in and of themselves, offer little increase in productivity. However, designed as an integral part of a total software production system, they could have sufficient impact to justify the investment in their creation. This is predicated on the assumption that the design of such a production system will imply or contain constraints about how programs should be expressed or structured.

- Minimization of the fraction of new code needed for each new application can have a marked effect. Reusable modules and the necessary supporting subsystems should be defined and tried.

- Better, faster, more efficient, and more effective ways must be found to transfer new capabilities, as soon as they become available, from those who develop them to those who need them. This is an extremely complex problem involving management, economics, and — far too frequently — personalities.

- The quality of software products must be improved from the stand-points of reliability, usability, and flexibility. Among other things, this implies improved ways of designing and testing programs, and it also implies getting the end users into the development cycle from the beginning and making them equal partners in the development process. It also means making both the developers and the end users accountable and responsible.

- An integrated view of the total data processing system, including the end user and his working environment, as well as the computer that forms the heart of the system, must be adopted. The benefits and detriments of the SCP-ICP concept, distributed data processing power, hierarchical storage systems, etc., must be evaluated as an integrated whole.

- It is questionable whether most of the following problems can be solved by 1985 (in fact, some may never be completely solved):
  - reliability of the *entire* data processing system;
  - installability of large on-line systems;
  - development of an SCP that is indeed inviolate;
  - methodology for the use of distributed data bases and computer networks;

- training and education (formal or otherwise) of data processing practitioners;
- development of programming into a technology;
- measures of the impact of data processing on the total productivity of the enterprise;
- improvement of the generally poor public image of the data processing industry.

REFERENCES

Bachman, C. W., and Bouvard, J. 1972. Architecture definition technique: Its objectives, theory, process, facilities, and practice. *Proc. ACM SIGFIDET Workshop on Data Description, Access and Control,* pp. 257-305. New York: Association for Computing Machinery.

Boehm, B. W. 1973. Software and its impact: A quantitative assessment. *Datamation* **19**(5):48-59.

Böhm, C., and Jacopini, G. 1966. Flow diagrams, Turing machines, and languages with only two formation rules. *Comm. ACM* **9**(5):366-71.

Brooks, F. P., Jr. 1975. *The mythical man-month: Essays on software engineering.* Reading, MA: Addison-Wesley.

Bylinsky, G. 1967. Help wanted: 50,000 programmers. *Fortune* **75**(3):141-43,168-76 (March).

Dijkstra, E. W. 1974. Programming as a discipline of mathematical nature. *American Mathematical Monthly* **81**(6):608-12.

Glaser, G. 1974. Keynote address, 1974 National Computer Conference. Montvale, NJ 07645: American Federation of Information Processing Societies.

IBM. 1953. Principles of operation: Type 701 and associated equipment, Form 24-6042-1. 1133 Westchester Ave., White Plains, NY 10604: IBM Corp.

Jones, J. C. 1970. *Design methods: Seeds of human futures.* London: Wiley-Interscience.

Knuth, D. 1973. Computer science and mathematics. *American Scientist* **61**(6):707-13.

Kosy, D. W. 1974. Air Force command and control information processing in the 1980's: Trends in software technology. Report R-1012-PR. Santa Monica, CA 90406: Rand Corp.

Maynard, H. S. 1974. User requirements for data base management systems (DBMS). In *Data base management systems (Proc. 1973 SHARE Working Conference on Data Base Management Systems),* ed. D. A. Jardine, pp. 129-45. New York: American Elsevier.

Poupard, R. E., Lee, W. H., Steele, T. D., and Hudson, F. J. 1973. Design considerations for shuttle information management. *Astronautics & Aeronautics* **11**(5):48-53.

7

MANAGEMENT

*I must be going now, for there go my
people, and I am their leader.*
Attr. to Mahatma Gandhi

1. INTRODUCTION

Much of the following material on management of data processing has
been foreshadowed in the preceding chapters; it is summarized and
documented here for emphasis and to present a unified point of view.
The topics included are:

- data custody;
- accounting for computer usage;
- management and data processing;
- vendor interfaces.

The significance of data processing in the large corporation has been
high for a long time and is still increasing. The current *direct* costs of
data processing run from less than 0.5% to 3% of gross revenues,
depending on the industry [McLaughlin 1976]. The direct data processing personnel (data input, operations, and applications development) seems to lie, on the average, between 1% and 3% of total personnel, but is significantly higher for some industries (e.g., finance). In
addition, the *indirect* costs of data processing include time spent by
employees who are *not* on the direct data processing payroll but who do
prepare computer input and use computer output; such costs are probably, on the average, at least equal to the direct costs and, in some
cases, are several times as large. There appears to be a shift of people
from direct association with data processing toward indirect (i.e., functional) usage. These trends are almost certain to continue between

now and 1985, not only in large enterprises, but also in small organizations, where data processing will become visible, for the first time, in the next decade.

A natural consequence of this visibility is management attention. A likely form of attention consists of imposition of controls on budget and personnel resources; a possible but less likely situation is one where management will examine data processing effectiveness and will look for missed opportunities. Even though not all data processing people report through the same chain of command (end and mid users are often separated from other data processing personnel), management awareness of data processing, as measured by the position in the corporate hierarchy of the highest data processing executive, has risen manyfold in the past twenty years to a level only a few steps below the board of directors. Even ten years from now, however, we expect that only a few enterprises will coordinate their data processing planning with the corporate outlook and strategy. This means that data processing staffs will still often be caught unprepared for changes in business lines, reorganizations, or substantially increased governmental reporting requirements. Management will notice and complain about lack of responsiveness but may be unwilling to pay the cost, in spare equipment capacity and personnel, for faster response to such changes. This lack of coordination and shortage of resources allocated to solving the management problems of data processing, stemming, in part, from a lack of recognition that one of the main tasks of data processing is to manage change, will tend to limit the growth of data processing—possibly even to an extent impeding the attainment of the economic projections given in Chapter 2.

However, the shift toward data processing appears irreversible and is making data processing services a critical resource of the enterprise. With the increasing integration of data processing systems into the operation of the enterprise, the consequences of data processing system outages become traumatic. Consequently, management will be likely to demand and pay for data processing system reliability and accessibility. And woe betide the operations manager who changes some part of the data processing system in order to reduce costs and, as a result, puts part of the company out of business for a few days.

The increased usage of data processing in the next decade will not necessarily cause organizational shifts between centralization and decentralization of authority and responsibility, but the capability of computer-based information systems will be used to increase the workable span of command for individuals. This increase could take the direction either of enlarged scope or of greater detail, according to management's desires. Similarly, there could be increasing variability of organizational structures for the data processing function itself. Small computers and terminals will very often be under direct control of the line organizations using them; large computers are likely to be controlled from headquarters as a shared corporate resource. Computer networking can be used to facilitate either centralization or decentralization, and project, functional, or product-line structuring of the data processing facilities. New structures can also be easily accommodated, such as a matrix organization where each employee reports both to a technical area supervisor for training and competence rating, and to an administrative supervisor for work assignment and productivity rating.

2. CUSTODY OF DATA

The function of corporate custody of data is best exemplified by analogy with a bank, which provides its clients' negotiable assets with physical safety against destruction, security against loss by theft, protection against loss through forgery, privacy in lock boxes and numbered accounts, ability to use such assets conveniently, and some integrity provisions against errors (e.g., the monthly statement). The custody of data requires similar considerations: safety, security, protection, privacy, usability, and integrity. However, the mechanisms used are different, since the assets, in the case of data custody, are information, and the threats to those assets can be both internal and external to the enterprise. Furthermore, there is no FDIC to protect the "depositor" if data are lost.

Five considerations become more important regarding the custody of data as compared to money or negotiable assets:

- Naming and definition are required for a very large number of entities.
- Ownership and access may be shared and controlled in complex ways.
- Integrity, security, and privacy provisions can become quite complicated.
- The cost of custody rises significantly according to the level of service supplied.
- The value of information varies with time, and may be different to its owner, a user, or a prospective malefactor.

Ultimately, data will be viewed as an asset of the entire enterprise, but the currently available hardware and software technology for supporting the custodial function is woefully inadequate to meet even present needs, and does not begin to cope with the more stringent requirements of the future. By 1985, we expect the technological issues to be resolved, in an economically viable manner, so that the cost of protection will be less than the expectation of risk from a rational malefactor. However, it will be very difficult to change practices and procedures to provide for the custody of data that is remote, either organizationally or geographically, from its owner. In 1985, we are likely to be in the midst of a complicated transition from data owners with direct custody of their own information to a workable separation of ownership and custody [Nolan 1973].

The accounting and auditing professions must develop and validate new principles and procedures suitable for data-base and data-communications oriented systems. The need is urgent and requires great emphasis. Real progress must occur; double-entry bookkeeping (a standby since the Medici in the 1400's), expenditure authorization and approval procedures, manual verification, and batch balancing with check totals are likely to prove either redundant or inadequate for on-line transaction processing.

3. ACCOUNTING FOR COMPUTER USAGE

Because data processing expenses are becoming a significant fraction of the total cost of doing business, many firms require internal charging for computer usage. The underlying rationale may be to motivate organizational change, to control costs, to force trade-off analyses, or a combination of these [Dearden and Nolan 1973]. Regardless of the motivation, it is desirable to separate the mechanisms for recording either the consumption of resources or the functions accomplished (or both) from the enterprise's policies ascribing monetary value or cost to these activities. This separation allows the forecasting of future resource needs and the control of the effectiveness of resource usage, independently from any incentive the enterprise may choose to use in order to influence the rate and kind of applications development. But it still leaves a number of thorny questions, e.g., how to allocate the costs of available but unused capacity, or of system and software overhead.

Resource accounting is becoming increasingly difficult and complex as the operating system redistributes resources and components among users in very small time quanta and in very complicated ways (e.g., overlapped, multiplexed, interleaved). Moreover, the resources used by a given job may vary from one "run" to the next, depending on what else is happening in the system at the time. However, the users expect that all the differences in charges for running a given job should be due solely to changes made by the *user* between runs, and that such charges should be predictable. Charges based solely on resource usage (even if computed with extreme accuracy) will not meet these expectations.

In a few cases, attempts have been made to relate the price of services to their "value" rather than to their cost. An objective measure of value is difficult to obtain, however, and it is not clear that value charging provides effective control for either the user or the installation. In any event, charging by either "standard" cost or value does affect the accounting system, but it does not obviate the need for detailed resource usage statistics. In the extreme case when the data processing center repairs "for free" a program that consumes an inordinate amount of resources (e.g., by "thrashing")—which is equivalent to the no-charge tow that removes a stalled car from the Holland Tunnel—such statistics are required in order to identify the offending program. The ability to gather usage statistics requires a measurement capability.

Another approach to pricing service is based on recording the functions performed, perhaps grouped as follows:

- computer instructions or programming language statements;
- system control program service calls;
- system commands;
- data access and manipulation.

To these must be added charges for the use of storage, connect time, etc. This functional accounting approach also gives information about how the applications systems are actually used, by pointing out the most frequently executed language statements, service calls, and commands. This kind of information can be of immense value in system tuning efforts and is necessary to control (even moderately well) an interactive data processing system [Boies 1974]. The vendors should help by defining and providing data collection means for functional and resource units.

From a technological standpoint, it may be desirable to use a mini-computer to watch over the main computer and to monitor faults, resource usage, and functions performed. The situation is complex now and is getting more so as various functions migrate from application programs to "supervisory" systems such as IMS [IBM 1973], and on to the system control program. For example, the system control program performs certain actions, such as paging, on its "own" behalf; it also performs actions directly attributable to, or "on the account of" a particular application or subsystem, such as IMS, under which may be running several completely independent application programs. Proper accounting may require the recording of the origin of each work request, and such a high resolution might be attainable at a reasonable cost only through the use of additional, programmable, and perhaps external hardware.

One might think that the charging problem disappears as hardware capacity increases and hardware costs per operation drop, but we feel that shared data bases, computer networks, and the rising cost of software will keep the issue of proper charging for data processing services alive for a long time to come in most installations. We do note, however, that a few enterprises have merged data processing services into general administrative overhead for accounting purposes; their users are not charged for specific jobs or transactions; but even in this situation, resource measurements are still used to control the operation of the data processing facility and to charge outside users [Luehrmann and Nevison 1974].

4. MANAGEMENT AND DATA PROCESSING

This section covers the topic of data processing management in the following order:

1. stewardship of the enterprise;
2. use of data processing in business functions;
3. computer installations and applications development;
4. administrative support services;
5. education.

The increase in the amount of data processing done in the enterprise, as well as the shift toward the integration of data processing into business operations, will lead to a shift of management attitudes from the nurturing of a new and strange technology toward the expectation of timely and dependable contributions to the profits of the enterprise. This is what management expects from any mature business function. In the past, the placement of the data processing function within the corporate structure has often been dictated by the business activity that was traditionally the dominant data processing user—the accounting or the engineering department. In the future, enterprises will give data processing the same status they give to other management functions, such as treasury, legal, accounting, manufacturing, and marketing. However, in the 1980-1985 time period, data processing skills are not likely to be a primary route to the top of the corporate ladder. Nonetheless, in some major corporations *not* in the data processing business, the boards of directors will begin to have one or more members drawn from the data processing field; we guess that there will be one or more chief executive officers with data processing backgrounds in some very large firms by 1985.

The data processing function appears to differ somewhat from the older business functions in that it is harder to compartmentalize. It will be used by *all* the other corporate functions; it is a service. It will be an adjunct to all of management, rather than a separate "piece" of management. Moreover, treasury or accounting departments seldom ask marketing, legal, or manufacturing departments about the extent or effectiveness of the treasury or accounting activities in the latter's respective areas; the older functions are, to a large degree, self-policing and independent. The data processing department, on the other hand, will probably ask questions of all other functions, regions, or product lines as to the effectiveness of data processing in their respective areas, and will *be* asked whether the total amount of data processing is appropriate to the enterprise's business.

It is probable that this pervasiveness of utility, coupled with old functional prerogatives and rivalries, will prevent data processing from remaining under one (or more) of the old functions. The natural home for data processing might be thought to be "Administrative Services," which provide the buildings, office equipment, communications, clerical services, etc.; but the combination of the high cost of data processing and of its integration into management's job of operational decision-making militate against this.

These conditions are likely to limit the growth of public data processing utilities in the 1980-1985 time period. The larger firms may have their own internal data processing "utilities," but they will probably be unwilling to risk moving so vital a function outside of their ownership and control. Some smaller firms may buy data processing services from outside (just as very small firms today buy accounting services, rather than have their own accounting departments), but in most cases they will be more likely to use "facilities management" services for their own equipment, or simply to do it all themselves.

Finally, we note that business has always displayed an amazing diversity of workable organizational forms. This will not change appreciably in the future—many forms of organization will exist, but we feel that the trend is toward an independent (and higher) status for data processing. Much of the remainder of this chapter will apply regardless of the organizational forms adopted for the data processing function within any given enterprise.

4.1. Stewardship of the Enterprise

The function of management can be viewed as having several components: the setting of organizational goals and directions, the acquisition (or development) of resources required to reach these goals, the allocation of resources among various goals, and stewardship over these resources. The last area, stewardship, tends to receive the greatest attention, partially because it is more understandable, and partially because it is easier to show what has been accomplished, at least in the traditional line functions of the business. However, management has not been very good at self-assessment: one seldom asks, much less answers, questions such as "What is the return on investment of the accounting department? Should that department be larger? Smaller?" Because of its expense and visibility, these are the kinds of questions that are beginning to arise with respect to the data processing function [McFarlan 1973]. We note parenthetically that the lack of assessment of the accounting function probably stems in part from the legal requirements for its existence.

The answer to the fundamental contribution-to-profit question for data processing will have to be partially supported with the usual evaluation and reporting tools of corporate management:

- long-range data processing forecasts and plans;
- accountability procedures, such as historical trend lines, and annual plan versus actual performance comparisons for the following areas:
  - equipment costs;
  - personnel costs;
  - research and development costs;

- applications development costs;
- services provided and their cost breakdown;
- compliance with standards;
- career development planning for key individuals;
- construction and use of indices of performance such as:
  - employees per million dollars of computer equipment;
  - normalized cost per (standardized) computer work unit;
  - data processing costs per professional employee within a function, region, or product line;
  - amount of production work as a function of total resources used;
  - support, maintenance, and improvements of applications as a function of total resources used;
  - new development or major extensions of applications as a function of total resources used;
- project audits;
- function, installation, and operations appraisals.

There is a real danger that the traditional management tools will not fit the needs of the data processing function very well, since they were developed largely for cost control of primary functions such as manufacturing. They do not focus on missed opportunities that could have provided added value to the enterprise, or on the question of what computers should be doing, and why. Such tools were developed for stewardship of areas with moderate rates of growth and change (where 10% per year is high) rather than the 20% to 30% per year growth and change rates experienced in data processing. Finally, these measures of effectiveness were based on ratios of people and money to the number of pounds of product produced or moved, rather than to the availability of more timely or better information. Improved utilization of data processing resources, if and when it does occur, tends to show up mostly in better results from the traditional functions, where its effects are combined with many other effects, and with the capabilities of the managers of these other functions. Hence we do not see, today, an easy way to isolate and identify the contributions of data processing to corporate profitability. Help in this area is needed, especially as data processing applications move away from the goal of direct cost displacement and toward improved availability of information. Means to measure "missed opportunities" within the data processing function (in the context of the enterprise as a whole) are also sorely needed.

These difficulties in assessing the value added by data processing to the enterprise have hindered the formation of a positive image for data processing in the minds of management. The applications systems to be produced in the future could assist in this regard. Operational control systems give a new opportunity to measure the productivity of corporate headquarters. Measures such as the cost of accounting per business transaction *could* be designed into future systems, and, to a reasonable extent, such measures *should* be built into those systems.

In spite of these difficulties in quantification, a number of enterprises will establish an "Office of Management Information Coordination" (or some such entity), which will have the task of relating information flow to decision making. It could set corporate policy as to what information, at what level of aggregation, and at what time, is to flow across which organizational boundaries. Not all data should be accessible to everyone at all times, even if it could be made accessible very inexpensively. In fact, added cost is often incurred to make access selective, as discussed in Section 6.2 of Chapter 2 in connection with information security.

4.2. Use of Data Processing in Business Functions

Serious difficulties in managing the data processing function are due to its migration toward the end user, as well as to the end user's rising expectations. When end users are located in the marketing department but can generate or modify applications, or when end users interface directly with the data processing system rather than with the people surrounding it, do they then count as data processing people or as "functional" people? To what extent does data processing skill enter into their performance appraisals? Does their computer-related efficiency, or lack of it, reflect back on the data processing installation or on their own performance appraisal? How are applications justified? Who pays for them? What cost basis is used for inter-organizational cross-charging? Who "owns" a portable application—one that is capable of being run usefully at a number of distinct locations within the enterprise? Who implements or acquires the various data processing tools needed to assist the developer? These questions and many similar ones relate to the unsolved problem of keeping benefits in the same organizational unit that incurs the cost. The statement: "You put in all the effort, and I will take all the credit" is not a very persuasive argument for getting work done. Yet there are general predictions and expectations of a great deal of growth in the areas of "integrated" data bases and applications. The unsolved problems alluded to above (as well as the restrictions placed by top management on the availability of capital for their solution) may prove, in some instances, to be the limiting factor to growth, rather than technical feasibility or overall economic desirability.

One way to avoid these problems without really solving them is to place all the responsibility for justifying an application on the function or department proposing it, leaving the data processing installation manager to supply the required capabilities at minimum cost. This does not, however, give management any help in determining how large the data processing activity should be, in assessing missed opportunities, or in setting the relative priorities of various data processing applications. Moreover, this approach makes it difficult to justify integrated applications crossing functional boundaries, such as those requiring a shared data base.

The structure of applications is changing, partly in response to the perception of needs for more accessible and adaptable data processing facilities, and partly because of new opportunities stemming from lower-cost hardware supporting data-base, data-communications, interactive, and local data processing capabilities. These needs and opportunities require much more complicated design trade-off analyses than were needed in the past, since benefits may depend on the implementation options chosen:

- local minicomputer vs. terminal to a central system;
- batch mode vs. interactive mode;
- local data validation vs. central control;
- specificity and compactness vs. generality and modularity;
- modifiability vs. reliability;
- etc.

Each such choice affects the way the computer subsystem interacts and interfaces with the personnel subsystem to form the complete application. Operating costs, development costs, and benefits must all be estimated over the whole life cycle of an application. When the system is installed, the users need to be made aware of the full functional capability of the application, and their managements may wish to measure their effectiveness in using that application. While a simplistic approach to data processing cost allocation may have been satisfactory in the past, when much of the justification depended on engineering or clerical cost displacement, it will prove inadequate in the future, when data processing may well affect the decision-making process itself. Consequently, research is needed to develop means for measuring the effectiveness and the value to the enterprise of the *entire* management function, as well as to develop measures of corporate productivity. If such research is successful, the results would assist in the quantification of benefits to be expected from data processing applications.

If the corporate decision makers and resource allocators do not gain a better understanding of the entire enterprise, of data processing, and of the interaction between the two (such understanding could come from the effectiveness and productivity research discussed above), then one or more of the following results are likely to occur:

- ill-considered integrated data-base applications;
- system configurations unsuitable for their intended purposes;
- inadequate or inappropriate integration of the data processing activities with the remainder of the enterprise;
- unfulfilled expectations.

4.3. Computer Installations and Applications Development

A data processing installation used to be operationally defined as a room full of computers and keypunches surrounded by mid and end users. The advent of IBM System/360 added large numbers of system support people. In the future, some of these rooms full of computers (as well as a sizable fraction of both the keypunches and the support staff) can and will be replaced by remote job entry stations and by end user terminals. Alternatively, such "computerless" work stations may be placed with groups that have never before had any kind of computer installation.

Such computerless installations might well be controlled organizationally by their end users rather than by the data processing center. This, in turn, might have a significant impact on the management style and career-path potential of those concerned with the operation and use of such installations. While the data processing industry has learned a little about how to evaluate the operations function of a "classical" data processing center, it has tended to ignore, in this process, the end users and applications developers surrounding such a center. Work is needed *now* to establish management criteria and procedures for appraising the computerless installation and for obtaining an overall evaluation of an installation that happens to also contain "classical" data processing operations.

The kinds of measures that would seem to be appropriate for such computerless installations are:

- its value to the enterprise;
- error and rerun rates;
- usage ratios: development-to-maintenance-to-production;
- responsiveness and quality of service to the end user;
- development-to-acquisition-to-reuse ratios of software modules that make up an application system;
- development productivity;
- usage productivity;
- hardware resources per person;
- end user acceptance.

In addition to measures that are believed to be meaningful both by managers and by their people, data processing installation management requires procedures to record both expectations and actual performance. This capability becomes a planning and control system through which a discrepancy between the desired objectives and actual results can (and does) trigger corrective actions. The principles of planning and control apply equally to *on-going* activities, such as generating the weekly payroll, and to *project* activities that have clearly defined start and stop points. However, a project is intrinsically more difficult to control because it practically never reaches a steady state. Existing development practices should be studied, but it appears that few installations today provide more than on-off (start-stop) control of projects, and many have almost no way of stopping a project prior to its completion or collapse. Better procedures are needed for estimating, monitoring, controlling, and auditing the development of applications.

As stated in Chapter 6, the development of application programs is today a craft; in order to manage it (as opposed to watching it), measures and expectations for quality and productivity need to be developed. Furthermore, training methods and procedures should be devised that are appropriate to the actual practice of applications design and development. Note that the fact that programming is a craft implies an apprenticeship or internship system, rather than purely formal training. The mixture of skills and abilities that is needed in a data processing function should be better defined and described (even though this mixture is likely to change between now and 1985), and both pre-selection procedures and post-performance evaluations of personnel and of results should be improved. The productivity of programmers appears to vary among individuals by factors as large as 10 or 20 [Boehm 1973]; remedial training and better selection could produce large overall gains.

Viewing programming as a craft is consistent with the observation made in Chapter 2 that loyalty to one's profession is increasing (possibly at the expense of loyalty to one's employer). This rising "professionalism" appears to run counter to the general erosion of the "work ethic" discussed in Chapter 2; but programmers generally seem to be highly motivated (i.e., willing to work nights, overtime, etc.), if only they have the needed data processing resources and meaningful assignments. At least today, the task of programming seems to give much satisfaction to its practitioners.

A major new problem arises with the maintenance or modification of on-line data applications. A "fix," improvement, added function, or version change is likely to bring the system or the data base down. In the old and current batch systems, parallel operation was possible for testing; reruns or fallback to a prior version were feasible. No such "insurance" exists today for on-line systems, and the various expedients now adopted are usually unsatisfactory. Installation and operations management must solve the procedural problems, and the vendors should provide help with the testing process, version fallback, and "parallel" operations in the context of on-line, data-base, and communications-oriented systems.

Between now and 1985, the interface between the data processing center and the rest of the enterprise, as well as the internal organization of the data processing center, are both expected to change substantially. Where many centers, in the past, were dominated by, or were captives of, single-client (i.e., functional) groups, the center of the future is likely to be impartially supplying a vast variety of services to different clients. A typical growth pattern is from local data processing only (data and remote job "entry" by mail), to remote terminals with the attendant communications network, to hierarchical data processing facilities, to computer networks with staged data processing and data aggregation, and possibly to a fully connected computer network with rather substantial general-purpose capabilities at many locations.

In a worldwide enterprise, the end users will be geographically, organizationally, conceptually, linguistically, and perhaps even culturally remote from each other and from their data processing installations. One should take care that they do not also feel psychologically alienated, since the concepts and culture of the developer of a system have an implicit but strong influence on its architecture. For example, a system built by plant designers may irritate plant operators, as well as prove to be hard to use for supervisors of data processing operations.

Instead of the periodic user group meetings that some centers hold now, there will be a need for a "data processing center representative" resident at each major user's site. Certainly hardware, software, and operational procedures must be improved, so that uncommunicated, inexplicable system failures become very rare, and failures of any kind are infrequent.

The volume of centralized clerical functions (keypunching, data input, and report production) will decrease as a fraction of the data processing center workload because of the decentralization made possible by source data capture, remote job entry, and on-line inquiry facilities. For the same reasons, the job scheduling and dispatching function will become largely automated, and operator-initiated recovery and reconfiguration procedures will become rare. Fewer lower-level computer operators will be required when (and if) tape and removable disk libraries are placed in on-line mass storage devices. Resident communications engineers may be added to the operations staff, as well as data-base custodians.

Operations managers will have greater overall responsibility than at present because of data custody and response time requirements, and they may have to make difficult allocations, in real time, of the remaining resources when the installation is partially disabled. They will probably provide 24-hour coverage of the data processing center by a responsible agent, such as a lead applications programmer, a data-base administrator, or both.

The system support activity is exected to move toward communications-oriented data-base applications as the vendors begin supplying generation, maintenance, and tuning services for the system control program (SCP), as well as language processors and other utilities (some of which they already provide, of course). The system support group will also monitor such things as machine loading and applications operating characteristics, in order to be able to advise center and installation management about the need to modify or upgrade either the hardware or the applications. Better measures are needed for forecasting the impact of prospective applications on overall system reliability and on the installation's spare capacity and loading.

Managers of data processing centers are likely to be more concerned with reliability and accessibility than with machine utilization. Catastrophe-prevention measures and recovery capabilities become essential as data processing is integrated into the main line of the business. Proposed hardware or software changes will be scrutinized carefully, certainly by the center manager, and in some cases by the end user, for impact on service, even if the changes promise substantial economies. Centers may have mutual backup arrangements, which will require establishing and maintaining various standards and network protocols; however, this will not, of itself, provide adequate backup. Even when resource sharing becomes possible, the phenomenon of the data being "down" will cause many an extended and expensive outage.

The range of future possibilities for procuring part or all of corporate data processing tools and facilities is hinted at (but not limited) by current practices in the use of facilities management, service bureaus, software houses, contract programming, and contract hardware maintenance. However, by 1985, large enterprises are likely to rely less on "outsiders," as these enterprises become more dependent on data processing for their day-to-day operation and survival. (This does not preclude cooperative use of data or programs within an industry, as discussed in Section 4 of Chapter 4.)

4.4. Administrative Support Services

The administrative services function is becoming more intimately connected with the data processing function. Joint planning involving these two functions will probably be a necessity in the future. This could lead to a merger of these functions in some enterprises, where administrative services become part of the data processing function, but we do not expect this to become widespread by 1985 because of the strong inertia of most organizations. It is even more unlikely that data processing services will be subsumed under administrative services, because of the integral and intimate connection of data processing to the operation of the entire business enterprise. Table 7.1 lists some of the parallels between administrative services and data processing functions.

The point is that neither administrative services nor data processing are ends in themselves; both provide functions that serve the primary purposes of the enterprise. Reorganization will stem in part from the realization of the commonality of many of the functions of these two areas and from the desire or need to integrate the services provided, and in part from the requirement to centralize the custody and stewardship over important corporate resources, data being one of them. For example, the realization of the "office of the future" (see Section 3 of Chapter 4), which is nearly possible today, implies either a replacement of an administrative service by a data processing service (see

TABLE 7.1

SOME PARALLELS BETWEEN ADMINISTRATIVE & DATA PROCESSING SERVICES

Services	Administrative Emphasis	D.P. Emphasis
Secretarial and clerical	Typing, "word processing"	Data entry, text processing
File and record storage and retrieval	Manual filing systems for reports, papers, microfilm, microfiche	Automated filing and information retrieval systems; manual and semi-automated storage and filing systems for tapes, cards, disks, listings, computer-output microfilm, microfiche
Reproduction and graphics	Reports, forms, slides, viewgraphs	Graphical input/output, computer-output microfilm
Equipment	Typewriters, calculators, dictation devices	Keypunches, data-entry units, interactive terminals, remote job entry stations, minicomputers, voice-response units, OCR devices
Telecommunications	Voice, messages, facsimile	Digital and sensor data, numeric information, text
Supplies	Stockroom disposables	Forms, cards, tapes, disks
Physical facilities	Office space	Computer center space
Assets protection and security	Physical assets	On-line information, physical assets

Table 7.1), or a combination of the two. Typewriters will be replaced by terminals, corporate files will reside within the data processing system, manual filing systems will be complemented or supplanted by data management and information retrieval systems, etc. As most keystrokes and other corporate data are captured and stored in the data processing system, today's generally held view that data processing systems are process-oriented will slowly but surely shift to one that

views those systems as data-oriented. These changes will dictate the nature and magnitude of the resultant reorganizations.

4.5. Education

One additional topic deserves mention here, namely that of the education of data processing personnel in general, and of data processing management in particular. Today, data processing managers are trained almost exclusively "on the job." In fact, some data processing managers have only scant knowledge of data processing technology.

We want to re-emphasize here[1] the fact that, by and large, educational institutions tend to concentrate on the more esoteric technical aspects of data processing, to the consequent exclusion of other, more mundane but very important, topics—those relevant to management, economics, data processing applications, system design, etc. This exclusion is also noticeable in many model curricula [CUPM 1964-67; Forsythe 1967; ACM 1968; COSINE 1968-72; Amarel 1971].

We do not wish to belittle in any way the importance of the "traditional" computer science courses (e.g., hardware, language processors, operating systems), but we feel very strongly that future data processing managers must be knowledgeable in, among other things, various areas of business (e.g., economics, organization of enterprises, management), in systems and applications design (e.g., implementation, planning, human factors), and in other broad, practical areas, in addition to being well grounded in data processing technology. The data processing industry needs the help of the educational institutions in this matter; the more recently published "ACM Curriculum Recommendations for Graduate Professional Programs in Information Systems" [Ashenhurst 1972; McFarlan and Nolan 1973] is a hopeful start in this direction. More substantive workshops, seminars, etc., are needed for the continuing education and growth of data processing managers.

5. VENDOR INTERFACES

The concept of mutual sharing of planning information concerning data processing systems and facilities between vendors and their customers is clearly desirable; a viable mechanism that protects proprietary interests and avoids legal complications is badly needed. Perhaps using

---

1. See Section 4.3 of Chapter 2.

a longer time horizon for planning than is common at present would alleviate these problems and offer less disruption of growth. The current long lead times for applications design and development often force the customer to make major decisions with respect to applications that must function efficiently in a hardware and software environment that is still on the drawing board.

If improved technological forecasting, based on better information flow between the vendors and their customers, were attainable, applications could be planned and justified on the basis of anticipated technology as well as on the basis of technology's status at the time such planning begins; the design of the applications could incorporate features designed to take advantage of the anticipated growth in technology.

In this area, we suggest that the vendors and the customers have a common interest as *users* and could profitably share their experience. The vendors should make more use of the fact that they are, themselves, substantial users of the hardware and of the programs they sell. Quality and productivity data from a vendor's own in-house users has, for that vendor, the added value of a market survey that helps the vendor's marketing strategy substantially. The vendors are better able than most of their customers to support major research and development programs in the areas of product quality, programmer productivity, and administrative problems. The results can aid everyone, but only if they are shared.

The remainder of this section discusses the various interfaces and interactions between the customers and the vendors in the following areas:

1. product packaging and unbundling;
2. standards and legislation;
3. concept transfer and marketing:
   - announcement and release frequency;
   - training and documentation;
4. maintenance:
   - technology;
   - policies and practices;
5. financing: rent, lease, and purchase;
6. user groups: function and value.

5.1. Product Packaging and Unbundling

It appears likely that the trend toward the unbundling (separate pricing) of software, peripherals, and memory is not reversible, and the buyers' motivation may change to emphasize quality, reliability, or specialization, rather than cost minimization. We believe very strongly that increases in total system reliability will be considered as being relatively more important than increases in functional capability, which in turn will have more relative importance than cost alone. The inability of a single vendor to supply all of the goods and services required for complex applications, and, to a lesser extent, economic factors, will lead more installations to a multi-vendor environment. As a result, data processing managers will gain confidence in their ability to deal with several vendors.

Major problems will occur in determining where interfaces should be located: is the input/output controller to be part of the central processor, in a separate unit, or integrated with the input/output device? Where does data management leave off and data-base management begin? However, the mid and end users will probably be insulated from such considerations, if only because these users will be too many in number and too unwilling to change their modes of operation. Exchanges of equipment are unlikely unless the effects of change are *truly* invisible to the end user, and probably to the mid user as well.

Attempts to encourage competition within the data processing industry are well advertised. One result may be quite stable, if not standard, interfaces at the hardware level. These trends will probably extend, with time, to SCPs. The "inviolate SCP" (discussed in Section 4.1 of Chapter 6) will necessarily—but with considerable difficulty—acquire stable interfaces. To accomplish this in a rational fashion requires much more careful separation and definition of the various functions and interfaces of the SCP (and of the installation control program—ICP—described in Section 4 of Chapter 3) than is the case today. The identification of common functions and the definition and packaging of software modules that implement them should be pursued both by user groups and by vendors. The success of the early SHARE library and the subsequent transformation of many of its program modules (as opposed to whole programs) into a scientific subroutine package illustrate the potential benefits that could be obtained in other areas of data processing.

5.2. Standards and Legislation

The development of standards is difficult in an industry that has the high rate of change shown by data processing in the last twenty years. Premature standards may block or delay progress substantially; they can condition the thinking patterns of great numbers of people for a very long time, as compared to the timing of advances in technology. For example, COBOL led many programmers to perpetuate monolithic design and programming practices, because modularity, subroutines, and structured coding techniques were developed after the original specification for COBOL [U.S. Department of Defense 1960]. On the other hand, deferring standardization for any length of time leads to a proliferation of non-interchangeable devices and languages, which ultimately will have to be converted, at great expense, to meet the eventual standards. A major consideration in standardization efforts should be to look at *entire* systems; viewing interfaces from only one side tends to lead to suboptimization, or even to conflicting functional specifications.

The customers, as a group, have the highest stake in standardization, but relatively few of them find the *immediate* benefits to them sufficiently large to justify their active participation in standardization efforts. This has left the standards field largely to the vendors, the government agencies, and a few dedicated firms and individuals. Direct customer participation in data processing standards activities is probably higher today than in some of the older areas, such as in standards activities dealing with screw threads or with the voltages and frequencies of power supplies; but we fear that this is a temporary effect, and that customer participation in the data processing standards activities may decrease in the future. This would be unfortunate, because the standards development organizations seldom contain a representative sample of current users. (A counter-balancing and promising trend is the participation of computer *user groups* and industry-oriented trade associations—such as SHARE Inc. and GUIDE International, and the American Banking Association, respectively, in data processing standards activities.) Compounding this problem is a propensity, in data processing, to develop prospective standards prior to the availability of demonstrable models of (and certainly before the existence of adequate experience with) whatever it is that is being standardized. Especially in dealing with prospective standards, it is all too easy to freeze the wrong things at the wrong level. (As an example, there are, at the present time, several efforts under way to standardize various job control and command languages.) Perhaps "end user" standards are needed, rather than those directed to the mid user or manufacturer.

The vendors who are active in standards-setting committees can (and sometimes do) vote in their own short-range economic interest, while many other users are often several years behind the forefront of technology and are thus unable to protect themselves. This situation is likely to continue until or even be aggravated by 1985; but the stakes involved are getting higher for almost everyone.

The most disquieting aspect of standardization is the fact that technological developments are occurring that permit or induce changes in the location of interfaces between components of computer-based information systems. It seems too early to tell whether the economics of changing the location of interfaces are significant in the long run, but the problem needs consideration. An example here is the same as that given for product packaging; namely, the decision about how much of the channel control function for disk drives should be in the disk controller, in a separate unit, or in the central processor.

The issues of privacy of data about individuals, of property rights to software, of interconnection to telephone networks, and of vendors' liability for data processing products and services, etc., are likely to be subjects of legislative action during the next decade. The user community should take care to educate the legislators about the costs, effectiveness, and benefits of prospective legislation from the data processing industry's point of view. Management should measure and examine the costs and benefits to their enterprises of direct action and of participation in user-group activities that deal with standards and legislative matters.

5.3. Concept Transfer and Marketing

More and more enterprises have come to depend on their vendors to introduce new data processing concepts in commercially marketable form, instead of performing their own research and development. This trend is probably characteristic of a maturing industry and is likely to continue. This will place a considerable burden on the marketing staffs of the vendors. Two problems arise. First, new concepts are intrinsically difficult to explain and to understand (to say nothing about the difficulties of effective use). Second, each vendor's marketing staff will find, or attempt to find, advantages for its customers in any concepts that its own organization develops or adopts. This partisanship further confuses the technology assimilation problems of the prospective user.

The so-called "independent" vendors seem to distract and even to confuse customers; but they render a valuable service by keeping the primary vendors "honest." They sometimes impede standardization (as in the current proliferation of data-base management packages), but sometimes they work hard for standardization, as is the case today with the manufacturers of plug-to-plug compatible hardware. Sometimes, a needed but unavailable device or program leads a potential customer to contract for research with an independent vendor, which may then be followed by cooperative developments within that industry.

Announcement and Release Frequency. Our feeling is that the frequency of SCP "releases" will diminish (or, at least, that the associated "release trauma" will diminish), since the growing use of on-line systems will preclude risking downtime for an SCP version change unless such a change is really essential. The rate of change due to IBM's System/360 and System/370 announcement and release frequency has been almost intolerable. The (badly underestimated) trauma of conversion to the System/360 has conditioned almost a whole generation of data processing managers to resist change unless the capability and reliability of the change are thoroughly justified and validated—preferably at some other installation. A key prerequisite for growth, from now on, is that growth be as *nondisruptive* as possible.

On the one hand, it should be realized that customer modifications to the SCP are a major source of problems; an installation permitting such modifications must be prepared to bear the consequences when a new version of the SCP is installed. On the other hand, a vendor must be able to guarantee that adequate capability is efficiently available in an SCP before that SCP can be made inviolate.

New versions of on-line applications system are more difficult to cope with than are new releases of today's SCPs. The customers have been put in a position of having to solve their problems in this area essentially on their own, but they really need the vendors' help to do it well. Moreover, both for applications and for SCPs, the customers must have *genuine* incentives to change versions, or version changes will simply not occur.

Independent suppliers are beginning to offer retrofit capabilities for aging hardware and operating systems in order to accommodate new functions that primary vendors reserve for new equipment. To the extent that this is effective, it may allow some installations to smooth out the technology assimilation process.

Training and Documentation. The already extensive vendor and mid user efforts in training and documentation often fail to meet the needs of users. Documentation is not equivalent to communication, but the vendors and providers of services all too often believe that it is. Currently, the situation appears to be worsening. The users simply cannot cope with another twelve or more shelf-feet of manuals per system. Systems will have to become much more self-teaching and self-documenting. It is clear that almost no users actually read all of the available and pertinent documentation, and that the majority of users do not attend the vendors' formal training courses. Formal training courses, in particular, have real limitations: quality, time, place, pace, and situation often leave much to be desired. The ways in which users are actually getting the information necessary to utilize new systems must be examined, and means must be found to do it more efficiently and effectively. A structured approach to design and implementation will help, but it does not solve this problem.

The problem of the effective transfer of information, concepts, and technology to the mid and end users constitutes a major research topic. Do users need "newspapers," audio cassettes, a personalized information service, or other means of obtaining information? The current situation constitutes a major bottleneck in the data processing industry. It is important to realize that today's "documentation" (i.e., shelves full of ill-organized and often outdated—if not downright erroneous—manuals) is often an impediment rather than a help in this process of transfer of information.

5.4. Maintenance

Technology. Maintenance of hardware is still unsatisfactory to most customers (owing to their rising requirements and expectations) and costly to the vendor. Substantial improvements have been expected with respect to hardware reliability from the processes of:

- packaging a set of individual components onto a "card";
- providing redundancy, so that the failure of an individual component will not cause the failure of the entire card;
- providing diagnostics to isolate a failing card;
- modularizing the functions performed by a card, so that failures on one card do not propagate to other cards.

Unfortunately, these developments have not yet improved the mean time to failure by the required two to three orders of magnitude, even though substantial aids to maintenance personnel are provided through the engineering consoles that display operating data, through preventive and diagnostic maintenance procedures, and through information retrieval systems for associating the symptoms of a failure with its potential causes. A recent improvement in this area is the ability to connect computers to a central test facility through dial-up telephone lines.

Developments in remote diagnosis and repair by module replacement (the latter perhaps even done by the customer) will continue, hopefully requiring fewer, less skilled field-maintenance people, and still producing significant improvements both in the mean time to failure and in the mean time to repair. The trade-off between this remote diagnosis approach and skilled, on-site field personnel is interesting, and its effects are not altogether clear. We expect that the emphasis will be toward fault-tolerant modules and on-line diagnostics (perhaps from an "outboard" minicomputer). This could result in semi-automatic maintenance of the hardware through continuous monitoring, and it could also help availability by automatically switching to alternate modules or data paths. Today's failure rates and times to repair will not be acceptable in the future, and they already severely inhibit the growth of many on-line applications.

Maintenance techniques for *software* are much less well developed than their hardware equivalents. No analogs to fault-tolerant modules or preventive maintenance methods have been adequately field tested, at least in general-purpose computers, and diagnostic procedures appear to be at a level approximately equivalent to the logic diagrams and oscilloscopes used for hardware maintenance in the late 1950's. Software repairability and fail-soft capability are still at a very low level. Hardware test points are costly, but software test points are even more expensive today (but tolerably so, if included in the original design). The capability to bypass failing areas of code is conceivable, but today it has to be invoked manually. We note that IBM states that new concepts in system design and implementation have been incorporated into its MVS SCP [Scherr 1973]; IBM recognizes the software reliability problem and hopes to reduce the number of errors and soften their effect in that particular SCP (as compared to its predecessors).

Software reliability and maintainability must improve dramatically by 1985 in order to support the increased requirements for reliability of communications-oriented data-base systems; some supporting technology appears to be emerging [Baker 1972; Parnas 1972], and we expect that it will be utilized. The concept of a "layered" operating system with a "hard core" (as in IBM's VM/370, where the control program deals only with scheduling and resource allocation, and all other functions are cleanly separated from it) appears promising, especially for interactive applications. Another possibility is our suggestion of providing an ICP, as discussed in Section 4 of Chapter 3. Investigation of problems of software reliability is a major research area; we doubt that an entire SCP that has truly zero defects is economically feasible today, or will be even in 1985.

Policies and Practices. We speculate that contractual provisions regarding system reliability (including hardware, SCPs, and program products) are likely to become more stringent, and more demanding on the vendors, owing to the increasing economic consequences of system failures to the customer. Will software guaranteed for five years command a premium over that with a one-year guarantee, or no guarantee at all? What does a software guarantee mean? Does it imply a penalty payment in case of failure? Loss of rental until the failure is fixed? A fix? An immediate effort to fix? A temporary fix followed by permanent repair in the next "release"? In order to cope with such added liability, vendors will probably impose additional requirements and restrictions on their customers. However, it may be possible for the customer to purchase one of two or more levels of reliability (and service) at different prices, just as one can do today in hardware, e.g., by duplexing the entire configuration or parts thereof, or by buying "hardened" or "ruggedized" system components.

5.5. Financing: Rent, Lease, and Purchase

Our view is that more enterprises (especially the large ones) will make wider use of the various available options with regard to hardware financing—some purchase, some "third-party" lease, some long-term rental, and some short-term rental, with the choices strongly influenced by the availability of capital. They will seek a "minimal maximum-loss exposure." Moreover, owing to the variability of tax, regulatory, and money-market effects, alternative financing procedures will continue. All plans, with the possible exception of short-term rental, will almost certainly *not* carry overtime charges, except perhaps for off-hours maintenance. However, the actual rates charged could vary with both the capability provided and the capacity used. An analogy is found in the complex charging algorithms used for industrial electric power, which account for peak demand, actual usage, and load characteristics such as inductance and capacitance ("power factor").

There are currently greater cost and time-delay step functions in acquiring additional data processing capacity than customers desire.

Perhaps this effect can be mitigated by metering and pricing separately for the capability provided and for actual resource usage. This might even be more economical for the vendor than delivering and maintaining different hardware models and correspondingly different SCPs.[2] Similar strategies could conceivably be applied to primary storage. With regard to software financing, some independent software vendors are already marketing their products on a metered basis (by transaction, by number of records sorted, etc.), rather than solely via purchase or fixed monthly rental.

Large step sizes, long lead times, and the incentive for long-term financing add impetus to hardware and software planning. Two major planning criteria are possible—one is to ensure that data processing equipment is fully utilized, and the other is to provide enough spare capacity so that adequate capacity is available when needed. It may be possible to minimize the conflict between these two criteria by using computer networks (should they prove viable) for load sharing at the large, interconnected computers, and by providing lightly loaded "intelligent" user terminals and job entry stations. This approach is somewhat analogous to having, in an enterprise, specific secretaries assigned to small groups of employees, as well as large, generally accessible typing pools. As is the case with secretarial services, the issue of the right balance between availability and utilization is likely to remain unsettled for a long time to come, and certainly beyond 1985. However, the decreasing costs of hardware, as compared to the costs of people and of software, will tend to promote the acquisition of spare hardware capacity. As an example, management today is, in general, more concerned that a desk or pocket calculator be available when needed than that all such calculators be used at least five hours per day [Boehm 1973].

5.6. User Groups: Function and Value

The emphasis within user groups has shifted from producing and sharing software and technical concepts to specifying needs that the users want the vendors to fulfill and to putting pressure on the vendors to do so. Members of user groups still do exchange fixes, "patches," and an occasional utility program, as well as, more recently, some cost, performance, and reliability information. The current emphasis is

---

2. Data processing folklore has it that the first instance of this occured in the 1950's, when an aerospace company rented an IBM 704 *without* floating-point hardware to replace two IBM 701's, but actually got one *with* floating-point hardware (so that diagnostic programs could be run) and a disabling, locked switch for that hardware.

on defining common-interest and effective cooperation areas for installations, user groups, and vendors, as this study attempts to do.

User groups still provide a technical forum where an installation's representatives can come to be educated. Our feeling is that this purpose is best served when the sessions (even if formal) are highly participative, with comments and argument from the audience. The presenter often gains new insight from the questions asked; and if the presentation is by a vendor, that vendor can gain valuable market-research information from the reactions to such a presentation.

As data processing enters the mainstream of corporate business, we fear that increasingly large fractions of software and of experience may become less and less shareable, due to the (real or imagined) proprietary interests of the owners of such software or experience. Such a trend would be most unfortunate, because it would impede the standardization and reuse of software modules (see Sections 4.9 and 5.2 of Chapter 6). We believe that real proprietary interests can often be served best by selling software or data processing "know-how" at an appropriate price, without resort to secrecy; this can be more beneficial to the advance of technology than giving software or "know-how" away. However, exorbitant pricing and unwarranted secrecy inhibit innovation and assimilation of technology. A *workable* solution to the problems of software protection would be of some help, as pointed out in Section 2 of Chapter 2.

As more and more people come to user-group meetings to "take" rather than to "give," the user groups run the risk of becoming less and less effective and useful. There is also a question whether a technically oriented group, such as SHARE Inc., can attract management-oriented attendees who can and will work on the problems outlined in this chapter. The problems are difficult and urgent, the solutions are likely to be widely applicable, and a collaborative approach is likely to be effective. We feel that these potential benefits can be made apparent to managements of user installations, thus assuring their participation.

The present and future value of user groups to installations and to vendors must be assessed by all concerned. There are common areas of interest between the user installations and their vendors that can be made explicit. Cooperation in such areas would have results with observable value to the vendors, to the user installations, and to the user groups. Of course, each must perceive the value to itself in order to continue its participation.

6. CONCLUSIONS

Because data processing expenditures (measured as a percentage of gross revenues or personnel) have reached, in large enterprises, a level of 0.5% to 3%, the importance of high-quality management of data processing resources is generally recognized; however, the required skills and tools have not improved to a satisfactory level. For a business function dominated by numbers, the data processing segment has remarkably little quantified information on how it uses its resources, and almost none on how they should be used. This gap between the need to manage and the ability to do so will probably be narrowed during the next decade, either by limitations on growth imposed by lack of credible justifications, or by improved capabilities for planning, measurement, and control. *Research* directed toward the development of better tools and *training* in the use of available methods are urgently needed. Users, user groups, vendors, and universities would all benefit from sharing their knowledge, experience, and needs in this area.

With regard to the stewardship of corporate data and data processing resources, new principles and procedures must be developed by the accounting and auditing professions to accommodate the changes that have occurred in data processing technology. In addition, organizationally sound practices should be developed for the sharing of data among geographically, functionally, and hierarchically separated units. Such data sharing complicates the already difficult problem of the suitable allocation of computing charges to end users.

The problem of identifying the contribution of data processing to the goals of an enterprise (e.g., corporate profitability) is shifting from measuring cost reductions toward quantifying the benefits of more timely, accurate, and consistent information. The solution to this problem appears to require measures of effectiveness and value to the enterprise of the *entire* management function.

The critical issues involved in the management and administration of applications development projects are the measurement and assurance of product quality (especially reliability, usability, and adaptability), and the measurement and improvement of developer productivity. For many applications, development and maintenance account for the bulk of total life-cycle costs; for almost all applications, the "people" costs are much greater than the "hardware" costs. Major improvements are needed in the data processing industry's ability to measure quality and productivity. Such improvements are also needed in the industry's ability to train people both for performing the data processing activities and for managing these activities.

The problem of the effective transfer of information, concepts, and technology from the vendors to system support, mid, and end users is a major research topic. The current situation (i.e., documentation by the shelf-foot) constitutes a major bottleneck. Systems will have to become much more self-teaching and self-documenting.

The issues surrounding planning information and product packaging are complex, and are unlikely to be resolved in the next decade. Legislative and regulatory changes of vital significance are likely to be proposed and enacted before 1985. Computer users and user groups should participate in these deliberations, especially as regards:

- guarantees of service availability;
- protection of proprietary software;
- flexibility in acquiring computing capacity increments;
- flexibility in financing options;
- location of interfaces between hardware components, between hardware and software, and between various software modules, packages, and systems.

REFERENCES

ACM. 1968. Curriculum 68. Recommendations for academic programs in computer science. Report of the Curriculum Committee in Computer Science. *Comm. ACM* **11**(3):151-97.

Amarel, S. 1971. Computer science: A conceptual framework for curriculum planning. *Comm. ACM* **14**(6):391-401.

Ashenhurst, R. L., ed. 1972. Curriculum recommendations for graduate professional programs in information systems. *Comm. ACM* **15**(5):363-98.

Baker, F. T. 1972. System quality through structured programming. *Proc. AFIPS Fall Joint Computer Conference,* vol. 41, pt. I, pp. 339-43.

Boehm, B. W. 1973. Software and its impact: A quantitative assessment. *Datamation* **19**(5):48-59.

Boies, S. J. 1974. User behavior on an interactive computer system. *IBM Systems Journal* **13**(1):2-18.

COSINE. 1968-72. Publications by various Task Forces of the Computer Sciences in Electrical Engineering Committee (COSINE). 2101 Constitution Ave., Washington, DC 20418: Commission on Education, National Academy of Engineering:
  1968 (September). Some specifications for a computer-oriented first course in electrical engineering (ED 024 608).
  1968 (October). An undergraduate electrical engineering course on computer organization (ED 024 607).

1968 (November). Some specifications for an undergraduate course in digital subsystems (ED 027 218).

1969 (September). Impact of computers on electrical engineering education: A view from industry (ED 062 133).

1970 (January). An undergraduate computer engineering option for electrical engineering (ED 062 134).

1971 (March). Digital systems laboratory courses and laboratory developments (ED 054 810).

1971 (June). An undergraduate course on operating systems principles (ED 062 135).

1972 (April). Minicomputers in the digital laboratory program (ED 062 941).

CUPM. 1964-67. Reports of the Committee on Undergraduate Programs in Mathematics (CUPM). Berkeley, CA: Mathematical Association of America:

1964. On the undergraduate program in computer science.

1965. A general curriculum in mathematics for colleges.

1966. A curriculum in applied mathematics.

1967. Recommendations in undergraduate mathematics program for engineers and scientists.

Dearden, J., and Nolan, R. L. 1973. How to control the computer resource. *Harvard Business Review* **51**(6):68-78.

Forsythe, G. E. 1967. A university's educational program in computer science. *Comm. ACM* **10**(1):3-11.

IBM. 1973. Information Management System/360—Version 2: General information manual. Form GH20-0765. 1501 California Ave., Palo Alto, CA 94303: IBM Corp.

Luehrmann, A. W., and Nevison, J. M. 1974. Computer use under a free-access policy. *Science* **184**:957-61.

McFarlan, F. W. 1973. Management audit of the EDP department. *Harvard Business Review* **51**(3):131-42.

———, and Nolan, R. L. 1973. Curriculum recommendations for graduate professional programs in informations systems: Recommended addendum on information systems administration. *Comm. ACM* **16**(7):439-41.

McLaughlin, R. A. 1976. 1976 dp budget. *Datamation* **22**(2):52-58.

Nolan, R. L. 1973. Computer data bases: The future is now. *Harvard Business Review* **51**(5):98-114.

Parnas, D. L. 1972. Some conclusions from an experiment in software engineering techniques. *Proc. AFIPS Fall Joint Computer Conference,* vol. 41, pt. I, pp. 325-29.

Scherr, A. L. 1973. Functional structure of IBM Virtual Storage Operating Systems part II: OS/VS2-2 concepts and philosophies. *IBM Systems Journal* **12**(4):382-400.

U.S. Department of Defense. 1960. *COBOL: Initial specifications for a common business oriented language.* Washington, DC 20402: U.S. Government Printing Office.

8

RECOMMENDATIONS

We are in the same ship, so we must
make every effort not to sink together.
Eisaku Sato

This chapter consists of:

- a summary of our observations and conclusions, and
- our major recommendations for action by the data processing community.

Our recommendations are *not* in the form of proposed solutions. We feel that there are not, at present, readily available solutions to most of the problems we have discussed. Rather, our recommendations should be viewed as a basis for establishing priorities for the activities that must be undertaken in order to obtain solutions to the problems that face the data processing industry.

1. SUMMARY

This study describes the environment and the requirements that the data processing industry will face in the period from 1980 to 1985. The primary purpose of the study is to identify the *demands* that will be placed on the data processing industry in that time period and, more importantly, to call attention to problems that require changes in *direction* and *emphasis* within that industry. Without such changes, the industry's ability to satisfy the requirements of *end users* may be severely limited. That ability is the *sole* justification for the industry's existence.

151

In the short span of twenty years, data processing services have become crucial to:

- the enterprise,
- the economy, and
- the society.

and are becoming more critical every day. Therefore, it is essential that the industry recognize the profound long-range implications of the current major data processing *problems* and *potential limitations*.

This study assumes a politically, economically, and socially stable environment. It forecasts that increasingly complex and changing requirements will be placed on the data processing industry. The percentage of the U.S. labor force that relies (directly or otherwise) on the availability of data processing services to accomplish its daily work will grow from 30% today to 70% by 1985. A substantial fraction of these end users will interact *directly* with data processing systems, specifying both the data and the functions to be performed on that data; the vast majority of these end users will not, however, be data processing professionals. Therefore, major improvements are needed in the user-perceived quality, reliability, availability, and adaptability of data processing systems.

The most critical problems the data processing industry faces are the productivity of the applications software development process and the quality of the end products of that process. Today, applications development is a craft, not a science or a technology. It is a team task, and a very complex one. The data processing industry, partly because of its rapid growth and relative youth, provides services and performs functions that it cannot properly measure, plan, or manage. It does not, today, possess the means to measure and predict the characteristics and the productivity of the applications development craft; neither can it measure the quality, reliability, cost-effectiveness, and return on investment of the end products of that craft. The capability to measure and predict such aspects of that craft must be developed. To date, however, the industry has not devoted the resources necessary to do so. Therefore, data processing management faces a severe test. Present management techniques cannot cope either with the increasingly complex technological environment, or with the growing user dependence on (and expectations from) data processing services.

In reviewing the developments that are occurring in data processing hardware technology, the study concludes that rapid improvements in data processing hardware will continue into the future; large increases in speeds and decreases in cost/performance ratios are well within the capabilities of continually developing hardware technologies. Hardware reliability, however, is a very serious concern. We expect that some of the future cost/performance improvements will be used to overcome the current shortfall in hardware reliability.

Industry standards and legislative issues will become increasingly important. At present, knowledgeable members of the data processing *user* community do not participate sufficiently in standards activities or in legislative deliberations. Participation in these activities by representatives of *all* segments of the industry is becoming increasingly crucial if standards and legislation are to be constructive rather than constraining factors.

Problems of education and technology transfer are becoming more severe. The industry must strengthen its ability to continually update the skills of its labor force and educate it in the use of the rapidly changing tools and techniques that will be required of data processing professionals in an equally rapidly changing environment. Another serious problem that faces the industry is the need to make its applications systems usable by the *non*-professional end users. The user interfaces of applications systems will have to be as unobtrusive and consistent as possible; they must become largely self-instructional. Today, the data processing industry does not have all of the knowledge necessary to solve these problems.

All of the above problems, and others identified in this study, will very likely limit the growth of the data processing industry in 1980-1985 unless they are solved. More importantly, they may cause the industry to fail to meet user needs. In view of the already critical and growing importance of data processing, vendors and users alike must recognize these problems and their potential impact, so that the necessary resources can begin to be applied to their solution.

2. RECOMMENDATIONS

Our recommendations are grouped under four major topics:

1. usability of data processing services;
2. productivity of the applications development process;
3. data processing management;
4. education, standards, and legislation.

Underlying most of the following recommendations are two basic problems. The first is that the data processing industry has not defined (and, in many instances, has apparently ignored opportunities to define) the quantification techniques and the basic measurement tools required to enable the industry to evaluate proposed solutions to perceived problems. The second is that the data processing industry, unlike most other industries, has not made it a practice to collect quantitative information about itself (e.g., dollar volume, supply, demand, employee productivity, populations of various classes of employees and of equipment). Establishment of base-line measurement techniques for the industry and the collection of quantitative information about the industry are prerequisites for the necessary research and development in most of the areas listed below.

2.1. Usability of Data Processing Services

One of the most often heard complaints about present-day data processing systems is that they are difficult or clumsy to use. These complaints reflect a general lack of proper consideration by the industry for the environmental factors that bear on the overall usability of these systems. The prime attributes of usability, *as perceived by the end users,* are:

- the quality of the human engineering of the interfaces between data processing systems and their users;
- the reliability and the availability of these systems;
- the adaptability of these systems.

There is need for major improvements of each of these attributes.

Quality of Human Engineering. User-perceived quality is the paramount criterion here. This quality is inadequate today; furthermore, users' expectations for quality (just as for all other aspects of data processing services) grow with time. The main criteria for the quality of data processing services are:

- adequate function and utility;
- minimization of end-user error opportunities;
- forgiveness of end-user errors;
- accessibility, i.e., more direct control by end users over the allocation of system resources;
- "minimum astonishment" behavior;
- simplicity, understandability, and consistency.

The industry needs to:

- develop measures for these criteria; then
- measure these criteria in today's systems; then
- develop new systems (or modify today's systems) for the purpose of improving their user-perceived quality; and then
- measure and evaluate the resulting improvements and their costs.

Such a feedback process should eventually provide the industry with tools and techniques for ensuring that the quality of the user interface can be maximized in future systems.

We also observe that poor quality is at least partially responsible for today's poor public image of data processing. Improved quality is a prerequisite for improving that image.

Reliability and Availability. No user must experience more than one interruption of service per month. *Total system* reliability (including the central processor, memories, peripherals, communication links, terminals, operating system, application programs, etc.) must be improved severalfold over what it is today. Occurrence of failures more frequently than once per month, on the average, will not be tolerated by users; as a result, if this level of reliability is not achieved, growth in many areas of data processing applications may be severely limited, and may in fact be confined to areas where such reliability is not mandatory. We feel that such a level of reliability is achievable. A desirable goal is to reduce the number of *total system* failures to one per year.

The industry must find ways and means of providing evolutionary and nondisruptive growth for all data processing systems and capabilities: hardware, system software, and application programs. This is particularly necessary for interactive, on-line, and real-time systems. The perturbations created in the past by successive hardware and software "releases" are no longer tolerable, yet continued growth and improvements in capability are mandatory.

It is most important that vendors initiate research and development projects aimed at finding ways to minimize the mean time to detect and diagnose a system malfunction, the mean time to repair a detected malfunction, and the mean time to restart a system, concurrently with their efforts to maximize the mean time between failures. Similar considerations apply to applications developers, vendors of communication services, and all who provide services to the end user. To the user, a system has "failed" when it is not available (for whatever reason), or when it generates erroneous results or information. Of paramount importance, then, particularly for on-line systems, is the ability to perform the maintenance and the repair of a portion of the system without shutting down the entire system.

Adaptability. The major cost of software, over its lifetime, is directly attributable to *change.* Therefore, software must be built so that it can be adapted with relative ease to changes in user requirements, in system configuration, and in allocation of system resources, as well as to system growth.

A variety of ways have been proposed to improve the programming process, and some of them have the potential to make software more adaptable. All are too new to have weathered the test of time. Therefore, efforts should be immediately started that are specifically directed at maximizing the adaptability of software while simultaneously minimizing the cost of exercising this adaptability. Some of the issues that must be considered are the trade-off between generality and specificity, the quality of program documentation, programming language limitations, separation of function (modularity), independence from data formats (and even, perhaps, from data types), programming style, and the retention of efficiency of programs (i.e., minimization of system resources required). These issues are fundamental to the programming process and fall within the purview of all (vendors and users alike) who depend in various ways on the production of software, as well as of those who are concerned with that process in more abstract ways. Although considerable research is presently under way on some of these issues, it is indirect and attacks only parts of individual areas; there is little evidence of a cohesive, organized attack on the problem as a whole. Given the relatively high cost of *change* as a component of the total life-cycle cost of a software system, it is imperative that a broad general attack begin on this problem as soon as possible.

Usability, Measurement, and Interfaces. All of the above considerations regarding quality of human engineering, reliability and availability, and adaptability lead us to conclude that, if there are to be significant improvements in the usability of data processing services, the industry must be willing to commit itself to a major technical development effort backed by strong management involvement. Means for quantifying quality, reliability, and accessibility of entire systems need to be developed as soon as possible.

The vendors, the individual installations, and the various user groups must begin the data collection and analysis relevant to the measurement of these system characteristics. From such efforts there will, hopefully, emerge a basis for measuring, predicting, and guaranteeing the performance, quality, reliability, accessibility, and availability of future data processing systems and services.

Improvements in all aspects of the usability of data processing services depend strongly on the existence of clean and controlled interfaces between the various parts of a data processing system, such as:

- between the system control program (SCP, also known as the operating system, or OS) and the installation control program (ICP);
- between applications systems and data bases;
- between the computer subsystem and the personnel subsystem of each application;
- etc.

The industry must devote resources to the tasks of defining, standardizing, and optimizing these interfaces. The industry must also devote resources to the effort of improving the overall adaptability of its software at a minimum life-cycle cost.

2.2. Productivity of Applications Development

Improving productivity is a critical and immediate task. In Appendix B, we give some quantitative data concerning productivity, and we discuss the effects that the current *levels* of productivity and the current *rate of increase* of productivity will have on the demand for and on the supply of software.

We believe that the productivity of implementors (i.e., mid users) could well remain one of the primary limitations to the industry's growth and to its ability to supply needed services. However, before the industry can be successful in developing methods to improve this productivity, meaningful *measures* of productivity must be defined.

Means of reducing the amount of (or even completely eliminating) new code in the implementation of new applications must be greatly improved if we are to attain anything approaching the improvement in productivity that we believe to be necessary. Improved methods are required for building modular software and for making known its availability for reuse.

Better methods must be developed for allowing end users to express their requirements and specifications to mid users in an unambiguous manner in order to avoid misunderstandings and loss of information. Today, such misunderstandings often cause enormous wastes of resources of all kinds.

Much theoretical and developmental work is yet to be done in the areas of very large data bases and of distributed data bases. This work should begin before the widespread existence of such data bases becomes a fact, tending to preempt potentially fruitful solutions because of the high cost of conversion.

The extremely difficult research that will begin to make software development more uniform and more disciplined must be started. Although software development is a craft today, it seems reasonable to believe that, like other areas of endeavor (e.g., metallurgy), which once were crafts but have since become technologies, software development could also evolve into a technology. This, however, will be a lengthy process, because most of the necessary knowledge remains to be acquired, and the dissemination of such knowledge, once acquired, to the existing craftsmen will also take a great deal of time. The industry cannot rely solely on evolution to solve the problems of the 1980's.

In order to improve the productivity of mid users, we must improve their tools and the ability of these tools to be used effectively with one another. Tools are needed in the areas of:

- project management and control (for reporting, analysis, and resource scheduling);
- design (for specifying objectives, for simulating applications systems, and for "customizing" them);
- development and implementation (for managing program development libraries, for controlling the source code and different versions of applications systems, and for coding and documenting the software);
- testing (for "debugging," generating test data, and for regression, functional, performance, and stress testing);
- evaluation (for analyzing performance).

The concept of a program generator, generalized to one or more application areas (e.g., inventory control, order entry) is likely to prove of value and should be seriously explored.

The reduction to practice of the concept of the Installation Control Program (ICP) described in Section 4 of Chapter 3 could be of material help in improving the usability of data processing services, the productivity of applications development, and the management of data processing resources. Such a reduction to practice will, however, require a great deal of development work.

2.3. Data Processing Management

The costs of data processing services have grown to the point where the data processing function is becoming more and more visible to the user organizations and to the top managements of all enterprises. Too little attention has been paid to assessing, in financial terms, the value of data processing services to the users' enterprises. Many of the basic concepts of cost accounting can be applied to data processing systems and services in order to demonstrate the resulting tangible reductions in the costs of handling business transactions and business data. Cost-avoidance and value-added concepts, as well as measurement of improvements in end users' productivity resulting from the availability of data processing services often are effective ways of assessing the value of these services to an enterprise. The industry needs to measure the values that can be measured and estimate the contributions where measurements are not possible; it also needs to do a great deal of work in developing new and improved ways to measure and make evident the value of data processing to the enterprise. This will not only improve the ability of data processing managers to manage and to allocate resources, but will also improve the image of data processing within the enterprise.

Particular emphasis in data processing management needs to be placed on improved methods for:

- planning for service and applications requirements, as well as for personnel and equipment requirements;
- managing the entire applications development process;
- managing costs and resources;
- allocating costs for services;
- auditing assets, funds, and information transfer;
- administering data bases and computer networks (e.g., ownership, control, and custody of data, and availability of data and services);
- responding to changing requirements for services, resources, etc.;
- assessing the contribution of data processing to the enterprise;
- measuring the effectiveness of personnel utilization and training;
- measuring the costs and benefits of professional involvement of personnel (e.g., in user groups, professional societies, standards activities).

Management of change is perhaps the single most characteristic aspect of data processing management. The short history of the industry is one of constant change with very frequent introductions of new concepts, technologies, products, functions, and capabilities. The data processing manager must introduce and support change throughout the enterprise and must manage change within the data processing organization. Planning is essential in an environment where change is such a significant, overriding factor. Planning is also much more difficult in this environment than in more stable environments. Relatively long-range (three-year to six-year) planning will be necessary in enterprises that hope to have high-quality, low-cost data processing services. Throughout the entire process of managing the constantly changing data processing function, a great deal of attention must be devoted to the problems of how to motivate end users to accept change, and either how to make it as easy as possible for them to adapt to change, or, conversely, how to adapt the required data processing services to the needs of those end users for whom change is, for whatever reason, either inadvisable or inappropriate.

The industry must begin to develop a methodology for the design of "total systems" that takes into account the way in which such systems and applications fit into the *entire* enterprise, what other systems (e.g., personnel subsystems) they must interface with, and how. There is a need, during the design of an application, to be able to quantify the resulting design trade-offs between, for instance:

- specificity and compactness vs. generality and modularity;
- adaptability vs. reliability;
- operating costs vs. development costs.

Techniques and procedures must be developed for:

- estimating;
- monitoring;
- controlling; and
- post-installation auditing

of the development process and of its products.

2.4. Education, Standards, and Legislation

Education, standards, and legislation, while strongly affecting the data processing industry, are not under the sole control of the industry; they are also strongly affected by others outside the industry.

Education. All segments of the industry must become more interested and involved in the problems of selecting, educating, and training data processing personnel at all levels. Many of the industry's current problems stem from its inability to adequately select, train, and provide the necessary foundations for the growth of its single most valuable resource: people.

A methodology is also needed to educate and train data processing managers—and *their* managers—to enable them to effectively manage the total data processing resource, to perform the appropriate cost/benefit trade-off studies, and to avoid pitfalls and fads.

Another activity that requires participation by the entire data processing community is the establishment of a better coupling between the community of users and suppliers of data processing, on the one hand, and the research, development, and academic communities, on the other, to ensure that:

- the efforts and activities of the latter are more responsive to the needs of the former;
- the means and methods of technology transfer and assimilation are improved; and
- the basic research problems of data processing are being adequately attacked.

The solution to these problems can take many forms; formal coupling between industry and the various research and academic institutions, as well as better communication between government-sponsored research and development efforts and the industry are only two of the paths to be explored.

Both users' and vendors' managements must learn how to transfer, in nondisruptive ways, new concepts, techniques, software, and hardware from the laboratory, through the development and manufacturing cycles, to the users in the field. Documentation and training, for example, badly need improvement. The present methods of accomplishing these transfers introduce disruption into already overburdened data processing operations. Ways must be found to smooth the transitions and yet permit timely use and exploitation of new capabilities.

Standards and Legislation. In the areas of standards and legislation, even more than in the area of education, users have not taken a sufficiently active part. The industry can no longer afford for them to remain passive. *All* segments of the industry must take an active role during the formative stages of standards and legislation if the industry, its users, and the general public are to obtain constructive support from these endeavors, rather than be stifled by them.

User groups and industry associations in general, and every user installation in particular, must become more aware of, as well as more deeply involved in, standards-making activities. They must not only determine the immediate and specific impact of various standards, but also be aware of the long-range and indirect effects of such standards and, most importantly, determine what should and what should not be standardized. Without user involvement, the vendors and governments will, by default, create standards in their own self-interests, which may or may not be in the best interests of the users. Measures of costs and benefits of such user involvement, which presently are lacking, must be devised in order to encourage user participation.

The legal and legislative problems of software protection, privacy, security, etc., will require the attention and active involvement of user groups, industry associations, and individual user establishments if the solutions to these problems are to be optimized from the point of view of the data processing community. Although the byways of legal and legislative processes rapidly become complex and difficult to deal with, defaulting to the various governmental agencies, or to other special-interest groups, could have far-reaching and potentially negative results. Again, measures of cost and benefits of the users' participation in such endeavors should be determined. The involvement of user groups in such legal and legislative activities should be directed at providing *professional* and *technical* expertise and education to legislators, rather than at lobbying in the narrow self-interest of such groups and their members.

3. EPILOGUE

By now, it should be apparent to the reader that we believe that the data processing industry as a whole faces many severe challenges. Its ability to respond to these challenges will determine not only what kind of future the industry will experience, but also, to no small degree, what kind of future post-industrial society will experience. The burden on the managements and on the technical people of all of the agents and participants will be heavy and trying for an extended period of time, but the potential payoffs are more than worth the effort.

The primary leadership role must, as it usually does, reside with the collective managements of the vendors, of the individual installations, and of the user groups. The challenge to all is to determine an optimal way to reallocate resources and to cooperatively share both the burden and the benefits of the investment in the research and development efforts that will be required to solve the problems identified in this study.

APPENDIX *A*

ECONOMIC PARAMETERS:

1970-1995

The following points should be noted in connection with the numbers displayed in this appendix:

- All dollar figures are in terms of 1970 U.S. dollars and, therefore, do not reflect the various devaluations and revaluations that have taken place since 1970.

- The U.N. definition of GNP is employed for consistency; therefore, the data for the United Kingdom and the United States do not accord exactly with domestically published figures.

- The various extrapolations have been smoothed and adjusted, and so do not represent exact extractions from the cited sources. This was done partially for consistency, but primarily because our objective is to identify major trends and to draw inferences from those trends.

TABLE A.1

POPULATION—WORLD REGIONS
(In Millions)

Region	1970	1975	1980	1985	1990	1995
Developed countries:						
USA & Canada	228	239	257	273	289	306
Western Europe	353	362	371	379	387	394
USSR	247	260	278	296	315	334
Eastern Europe	104	108	112	115	119	122
Japan	102	107	111	116	119	123
Subtotal	1,034	1,076	1,129	1,179	1,229	1,279
Underdeveloped countries:						
Latin America	271	313	362	417	474	533
Middle East & North Africa. .	163	187	216	248	282	318
China	826	903	975	1,052	1,122	1,197
Asia[a]	1,100	1,245	1,410	1,580	1,740	1,930
Black Africa	238	267	305	346	399	457
Subtotal	2,598	2,915	3,268	3,643	4,017	4,435
Other	62	72	80	89	100	113
World total	3,694	4,063	4,477	4,911	5,346	5,827
USA only	206	215	231	245	259	273

a. Excluding China & Japan.

SOURCE: *U.N. monthly bulletin of statistics.* June 1968.

TABLE A.2

GROSS NATIONAL PRODUCT—WORLD REGIONS
(In Billions of 1970 U.S. Dollars)

Region	1970	1975	1980	1985	1990	1995
Developed countries:						
USA & Canada	1,093	1,363	1,688	2,121	2,653	3,307
Western Europe	745	925	1,130	1,400	1,720	2,140
USSR	448	572	730	934	1,190	1,520
Eastern Europe	167	214	274	349	446	570
Japan	143	204	294	376	480	613
Subtotal	2,596	3,278	4,116	5,180	6,489	8,150
Underdeveloped countries:						
Latin America	127	155	193	239	299	374
Middle East & North Africa..	52	67	86	110	141	179
China	123	178	242	338	475	665
Asia[a]	162	204	252	311	381	476
Black Africa	30	37	46	57	70	87
Subtotal	494	641	819	1,055	1,366	1,781
Other	64	77	96	119	149	185
World total	3,154	3,996	5,031	6,354	8,004	10,116
USA only[b]	1,020	1,270	1,570	1,970	2,460	3,060

a. Excluding China & Japan.
b. U.N. definition of GNP.

SOURCE: *U.N. monthly bulletin of statistics.* June 1968.

TABLE A.3

GROSS NATIONAL PRODUCT PER CAPITA—WORLD REGIONS
(In 1970 U.S. Dollars)

Region	1970	1975	1980	1985	1990	1995
Developed countries:						
USA & Canada	4,790	5,700	6,570	7,770	9,180	10,800
Western Europe	2,110	2,555	3,050	3,690	4,440	5,430
USSR	1,815	2,200	2,625	3,160	3,780	4,550
Eastern Europe	1,605	1,980	2,445	3,030	3,750	4,670
Japan	1,400	1,905	2,650	3,240	4,030	4,980
Average[a]	2,510	3,050	3,650	4,390	5,280	6,370
Underdeveloped countries:						
Latin America	469	495	533	573	631	702
Middle East & North Africa..	319	358	398	444	500	563
China.....................	149	197	248	321	423	556
Asia[b]	147	164	179	197	219	247
Black Africa	126	139	151	165	175	190
Average[a]	190	220	251	290	340	402
Other........................	1,030	1,070	1,200	1,335	1,490	1,635
World average[a]	854	984	1,125	1,295	1,495	1,735
USA only	4,950	5,910	6,800	8,040	9,500	11,200

a. Weighted.
b. Excluding China & Japan.
SOURCE: Tables A.1 & A.2.

TABLE A.4
INDICES OF U.S. LABOR EFFECTIVENESS

Index	1970	1975	1980	1985	1990	1995
Employed (in millions)	81.2	88.7	95.0	100.0	105.3	113.5
Mean work week (in hours)....	38.3	37.8	37.2	36.7	36.0	35.2
Hours worked[a]...............	3.11	3.35	3.53	3.67	3.79	4.00
Output per man-hour[b].........	1.00	1.15	1.35	1.63	1.97	2.32
Total output[b]	1.00	1.24	1.53	1.92	2.40	2.98
GNP per man-year[c]	12.6	14.3	16.5	19.7	23.4	27.0

a. In billions per week.
b. Normalized to 1970.
c. In thousands of 1970 U.S. dollars.
SOURCE: *Statistical abstracts of the United States.* U.S. Department of Commerce, 1970.

TABLE A.5
U.S. LABOR DISTRIBUTION BY INDUSTRY
(In Millions)

Industry	1970	1975	1980	1985	1990	1995
Agriculture	3.0	2.9	2.4	2.0	1.8	1.7
Mining......................	0.6	0.6	0.5	0.5	0.5	0.5
Manufacturing...............	18.9	19.8	20.2	20.5	20.8	21.0
Construction	3.6	3.9	4.0	4.7	5.0	5.3
Transportation & utilities	4.3	4.6	4.8	4.9	5.3	5.6
Trade	17.5	19.8	22.4	23.6	25.0	27.8
Finance & real estate..........	3.4	3.8	4.2	4.5	5.0	5.5
Services.....................	15.6	17.9	20.0	21.4	22.1	24.7
Government..................	14.3	15.4	16.5	17.9	19.8	21.4
Total employed	81.2	88.7	95.0	100.0	105.3	113.5
Government (breakdown):						
Military	3.1	3.0	2.9	3.0	3.1	3.1
Civilian Federal	2.8	2.8	2.9	3.0	3.2	3.3
State & local[a]	4.3	5.1	5.9	6.7	7.9	9.0
Education	4.1	4.5	4.8	5.2	5.6	6.0
Total government	14.3	15.4	16.5	17.9	19.8	21.4

a. Excluding public education.
SOURCE: *Statistical abstracts of the United States.* U.S. Department of Commerce, 1966.

TABLE A.6

U.S. GNP—MAJOR COMPONENTS
(In Billions of 1970 U.S. Dollars)

Component	1970	1975	1980	1985	1990	1995
Personal consumption:						
Durables	99	130	170	222	290	379
Non-durables	279	328	386	455	535	630
Services	269	347	439	573	735	931
Subtotal	647	805	995	1,250	1,560	1,940
Domestic investment:						
Residential structures	37	44	53	63	77	92
Other structures	38	48	60	77	96	120
Producer durables	76	96	120	151	191	241
Change in inventory	8	10	12	15	19	24
Subtotal	159	198	245	306	383	477
Government purchases:						
Federal	84	97	110	132	156	182
State & local	120	157	204	262	336	430
Subtotal	204	254	314	394	492	612
Net exports	10	13	16	20	25	31
Total U.S. GNP	1,020	1,270	1,570	1,970	2,460	3,060

SOURCE: *Statistical abstracts of the United States.* U.S. Department of Commerce, 1971.

APPENDIX *B*

GROWTH PARAMETERS OF THE

DATA PROCESSING INDUSTRY

Predictions concerning the growth of the data processing industry have been historically on the low side, and often dramatically so. It is a cliché to comment that the development of data processing has been explosive in all dimensions. This observation, however, is only a half truth. Certainly, progress in improving the cost/performance ratio of basic hardware has been dramatic. The total growth of the industry in terms of total annual expenditure is also impressive. On the other hand, improvements in such areas as programmer productivity and system reliability are not keeping pace with other developments. In this appendix we attempt to document the various available measures of the growth of the data processing industry in order to quantify, as best we can, the significant characteristics of that industry.

There is considerable difficulty in collecting and systematizing data about the data processing industry. The various industry reports and surveys found in the literature are not consistent, and sometimes not even self-consistent. Part of the difficulty is easy to find. As we have observed elsewhere in this study, there is a serious need for definitions of many of the measurable characteristics of data processing. For example, from the published material it is often difficult, or even impossible, to determine where divisions are made between "computers" and "minicomputers," between "programmers" and "system analysts," or between "research" and "development." In what follows, we have attempted to use sources least subject to systematic bias, avoiding, for instance, reports whose purpose is to show that minicomputers are taking over the world. In addition, we have tried to employ consistent interpretations of the terminology used. Despite all possible caution on our part, the numbers we provide should be used with great care. For our purposes, it is the *major trends* and the *magnitudes of the ratios* that are significant.

Growth of the Industry. The total annual expenditure for data processing is given by Gilchrist and Weber [1973] as 23.6 billion dollars for the United States in 1971. Assuming that Canada spends at the same rate as the United States (as a fraction of its GNP), and using the figures provided by Jéquier [1968] for the ratio between the total U.S. expenditure and the combined expenditures of the United Kingdom and the European Economic Community (as it was constituted in 1968), and extrapolating this ratio to 1971, we obtain a total worldwide expenditure of approximately 32 billion dollars in 1971, ignoring, for lack of data, Eastern Europe and the USSR.

The estimates [Gilchrist and Weber 1973] for 1976, when averaged, indicate a doubling of these figures over a five-year period. We are assuming, in the absence of data to the contrary, that these figures are in constant dollars. Earlier figures, derivable from Weik [1957], Weik [1961], and Jéquier [1968], yield substantially higher growth *rates* for the infancy of the industry. This early explosive growth was a start-up transient and is no longer pertinent; large users cannot increase their expenditures for data processing in an effective manner any faster than they are currently doing, given their already substantial data processing base. The current growth rate for *large* installations is just under 10% per year.

Examination of the results of the GUIDE/IBM Delphi Study [Wylie 1971] provides an indication of the expected growth of the data processing industry as a result of the introduction of *new* applications. Over 75% of the respondents in that study predicted 1985 or earlier as the implementation date for 96 of the 108 applications analyzed therein. An estimate of the requirements for data processing systems necessary to implement these applications leads to an approximate doubling of the dollar value of today's installed base by 1985 [Steel 1974]. Combining this and the previous analyses indicates, again, a five-year doubling time for the data processing industry as a whole. Tabulating these results, and extrapolating them to 1985, we obtain Table B.1. On the basis of the available evidence, we are reasonably confident of the realism of these figures.

Computer and Programmer Populations. The historical and extrapolated trends of the numbers of computers and of programmers are shown in Table B.2 for comparison with the expenditure data of Table B.1.

TABLE B.1

TOTAL DATA PROCESSING INDUSTRY EXPENDITURES

Year	USA[a]	% of GNP	World[a,b]	% of GWP
1970	21	2.1	28	.9
1975	41	3.2	56	1.4
1980	82	5.2	111	2.2
1985	164	8.3	223	3.5

a. In billions of 1970 U.S. dollars.
b. Understated because Eastern Europe & USSR are not included.

Two points concerning Table B.2 are worth noting. First, it is not clear whether the number of programmers, as extrapolated by us to 1985, is believable, but it reflects the growth rate of the past five years. Second, the diminishing ratio of programmers to computers appears to be real, although its lower bound is impossible to predict.

TABLE B.2

U.S. COMPUTER & PROGRAMMER CENSUS

Year	Computers			Programmers	P/GP[a]	P/T[b]
	Gen.-Purp.	Dedicated	Total			
1955[c]...	1,000	0	1,000	10,000	10	10
1960 ...	5,000	500	5,500	30,000	6	5.5
1965 ...	20,000	2,500	22,500	80,000	4	3.6
1970 ...	45,000	25,000	70,000	165,000	3.7	2.4
1975 ...	75,000	150,000	225,000	220,000	2.9	.98
1980 ...	125,000	575,000	700,000	275,000	2.2	.39
1985 ...	175,000	925,000	1,100,000	330,000	1.9	.30

a. Number of programmers divided by number of general-purpose computers.
b. Number of programmers divided by total number of computers.
c. 1955 data are highly uncertain.

Programmer Productivity. The programmer productivity data given in Table B.3 are derived from several sources and observations. It is demonstrable, even from the limited data available, that programmer productivity doubled from 1955 to 1965, and that most of the growth occurred in the first five years. It has been publicly observed that programmer productivity has increased by one-third between 1965 and

1975[1] (which is equivalent to approximately 3% per year, compounded), and one estimate, quoting a large aerospace company [Boehm 1973], corroborates our value for 1973. Our extrapolation to 1985 assumes that the 3% compounded productivity improvement per year will be maintained, all other things being equal. The indices in Table B.3 for programmer productivity and total production were derived from those observations and from the data of Table B.2.

TABLE B.3

PROGRAMMER PRODUCTIVITY & TOTAL
U.S. YEARLY CODE PRODUCTION
(Normalized to 1955)

Year	Productivity[a]	Production
1955	1	1
1960	1.6	5
1965	2.0	16
1970	2.3	38
1975	2.7	59
1980	3.1 (4.3)	85 (118)
1985	3.6 (7.0)	119 (231)

a. Assumes a 3% annual growth rate of programmer productivity since 1965; figures in parentheses assume a 10% annual growth rate of programmer productivity after 1975.

If these figures reflect reality, and if the numbers given in Section 1 of Chapter 5, which indicate as much as a factor-of-ten improvement in the cost/performance ratio of hardware every five years (which is equivalent to 60% per year compounded) are also realistic, we have a demonstration that programmer productivity is a potential bottleneck to further growth of data processing. Table B.3 also demonstrates that this conclusion holds even if the yearly improvement in programmer productivity were to suddenly jump from 3% to 10%, an event we consider highly unlikely.

System Reliability. As noted in Section 6.3 of Chapter 2, *system* reliability is less than optimum today. In view of the significant differences between current operating practices and those of twenty years ago, it is difficult to make accurate comparisons of system reliability. However,

1. Address by John F. Akers at the General Meeting of GUIDE International, 6 Nov. 1974.

analysis of reports [Jones 1956] concerning IBM 701 and 704 performance indicates a mean time between failures due to all causes of about one-half hour. Current experience [Reynolds and Van Kinsbergen 1975] indicates a comparable measure to be approximately twelve hours, yielding an improvement by a factor of 24 over a period of just under two decades. Extrapolating this improvement factor to 1985 gives a mean time to failure of approximately 60 hours. We believe this to be inadequate.

Summarizing the above figures, and considering only the decade intervals between 1955 and 1985, we obtain Table B.4, using 1955 data as unit indices.

TABLE B.4

SUMMARY OF DATA PROCESSING INDUSTRY TRENDS
(Normalized to 1955)

Indicator	1955	1965	1975	1985
Industry growth	1	20	80	320
Performance/cost	1	10^2	10^4	10^6
Programmer productivity	1	2.0	2.7	3.6
System reliability	1	5	24	120

Resources for Research. The availability of research funds is a critical element that limits the data processing industry's ability to rectify the imbalance between the performance of the hardware and the performance of the software. Taking data from Starr and Rudman [1973], if we use a long base line (1920-1965), *total* research and development (R&D) funds in the United States as a percent of the GNP have risen (with some fluctuations) exponentially from 0.2% (1920) to 4.0% (1965), with the 1950 point being substantially below the trend line, the 1960 point being substantially above it, and the 1965 point being right on that line. Taking a short base line (1950-1965), on the other hand, leads to a curve that peaks out at about 1970 and then plummets. Does the short base line result really represent what we can expect, or is it just a temporary R&D recession? The answer is as yet unknown.[2] The long-term decline in the *rate* of increase between 1930 and 1950

2. A recent report [National Science Board 1975] suggests that the downturn in total U.S. R&D expenditures as a fraction of the U.S. GNP may be a lasting phenomenon. However, there is, as yet, no evidence that this downturn has significantly affected data processing R&D.

was a consequence of the depression and of World War II. The upsurge between 1950 and 1965 was a consequence of the sudden glamour of science in the wake of the discovery of radar and of nuclear energy, the Korean War, and the space program (the last strongly stimulated by Sputnik). The present downturn appears to be a consequence of the disenchantment due to the Vietnam War, public apathy toward further space exploration, and a plethora of social ills whose solution is given, by many, a higher priority than science.

The complexities are obvious: a patriotic and total war means less R&D; a patriotic but limited war means more R&D; a questionable, limited war means less R&D. The public is fickle: science can mean "glamour" or "taking food from the poor." This public-attitude problem affects not only the Congress; it also infects the board rooms, albeit less drastically. It is quite possible that the resource-availability-versus-quality-of-life dilemma, so dramatically in focus at the time of this writing, will cause an upturn in the availability of R&D funds.

In the absence of more definitive data, we will assume that the 1965-1970 fraction of the U.S. GNP that is spent on R&D (4%) is a constant applicable beyond 1970. Applying this fraction to the figures of the last line of data in Table A.2, we derive the figures shown in Table B.5. The figure in this table for 1985 is not very meaningful for our study because of the "seven-year rule" mentioned in Chapter 1, but the key point is that, if the fraction of the U.S. GNP spent on R&D does remain constant in the future, the amount of R&D funds will grow exponentially.

TABLE B.5

TOTAL U.S. R&D EXPENDITURES
(In Billions of 1970 U.S. Dollars)

1970	1975	1980	1985
41	51	63	79

A rough measure of the separation between research on the one hand, and development on the other, can be derived from the changing ratio of scientists to engineers [Starr and Rudman 1973]. In the United States, there were 400 scientists and 2,000 engineers per million population in 1930, with an exponential rise to 2,500 scientists and 4,000 engineers per million in 1970. Assuming that the ratio of scientists to engineers is a reasonable measure of the ratio of research effort to development effort, then it follows that the ratio of research effort to development effort has increased by just over a factor of 3 between 1930 and 1970. We assume for the purposes of this analysis that these ratios remain constant beyond 1970.

TABLE B.6

1970 U.S. DATA PROCESSING R&D
EXPENDITURES BY CATEGORY
(In Millions of 1970 U.S. Dollars)

Data processing industry	800
Other industry...................	50
Department of Defense	160
Other.........................	10
Total	1,020

Reliable data about the fraction of total R&D money devoted to data processing R&D is difficult to obtain, but combining various estimates leads to an approximate figure of 2.5%. The approximate 1970 breakdown of that fraction by sector of the economy is given in Table B.6. The result is a figure of 0.1% of the GNP devoted to data processing R&D. Applying this percentage to the figures of the last line of data of Table A.2 gives the figures in Table B.7.

TABLE B.7

U.S. DATA PROCESSING R&D
EXPENDITURES
(In Millions of 1970 U.S. Dollars)

1970	1975	1980	1985
1,020	1,270	1,570	1,970

Performing a similar calculation for personnel resources (again using data from Starr and Rudman [1973]) leads to the figures in Table B.8,[3] and applying the same 2.5% fraction of data processing R&D to total R&D that we used to derive Table B.6 gives the results of Table B.9.

---

3. The National Science Board [1975] report cited earlier appears to support the data shown in Table B.8 for 1970 and 1975, but casts some doubt upon the projections given in that table for 1980 and 1985.

TABLE B.8

TOTAL U.S. R&D PERSONNEL
(In Thousands)

Classification	1970	1975	1980	1985
Research scientists..........	515	544	578	613
Development engineers	824	870	924	980
Total	1,339	1,414	1,502	1,593

The present estimated resource levels, 1.27 billion dollars and 35,400 people, should be adequate *if they are used properly.* A number of problems toward whose solutions these resources should be applied are identified throughout this study.

TABLE B.9

U.S. DATA PROCESSING R&D
PERSONNEL
(In Thousands)

1970	1975	1980	1985
33.5	35.4	37.6	39.8

Conclusion. In concluding this appendix, we must emphasize the uncertainty of most of the data presented here. Only the *trends* and the *order of magnitude* of the values are at all dependable. However, because the problems we have identified are in fact due to trends and to order-of-magnitude differences between what is and what should be, we believe that our major conclusions are valid independently of the large probable errors in these values.

REFERENCES

Boehm, B. W. 1973. The high cost of software. In *Proc. Symposium on the High Cost of Software,* ed. J. Goldberg, pp. 27-40. Menlo Park, CA 94025: Stanford Research Institute. Distributed by the National Technical Information Service (NTIS), U.S. Dept. of Commerce, Arlington, VA 22217 (AD 777 121).

Gilchrist, B., and Weber, R. E. 1973. *The state of the computer industry in the United States: Data for 1971 and projections for 1976.* Montvale, NJ 07645: American Federation of Information Processing Societies.

Jéquier, N. 1968. Gaps in technology between member countries. Report on the electronic computer sector. OECD Report DAS/SPR/68.22. Paris: Organization for Economic Cooperation and Development.

Jones, F. 1956. Letters to SHARE membership. Various dates from October 1955 through July 1956 (out of print).

National Science Board. 1975. *Science indicators 1974.* Report of the National Science Board of the National Science Foundation. Washington, DC 20402: U.S. Government Printing Office.

Reynolds, C. H., and Van Kinsbergen, J. E. 1975. Tracking reliability and availability. *Datamation* **21**(11):106-16.

Starr, C., and Rudman, R. 1973. Parameters of technological growth. *Science* **182**:358-64.

Steel, T. B., Jr. 1974. Data base systems: Implications for commerce and industry. In *Data base management systems (Proc. 1973 SHARE Working Conference on Data Base Management Systems),* ed. D. A. Jardine, pp. 219-34. New York: American Elsevier.

Weik, M. H. 1957. A second survey of domestic electronic digital computing systems. BRL Report 1010. Aberdeen, MD 21001: Ballistics Research Laboratory.

———. 1961. A third survey of domestic electronic digital computing systems. BRL Report 1115. Aberdeen, MD 21001: Ballistics Research Laboratory.

Wylie, K. 1971. Summary of results: GUIDE/IBM study of advanced applications. 111 E. Wacker Dr., Chicago, IL 60601: GUIDE International.

ADDITIONAL BIBLIOGRAPHY

This bibliography lists a representative sample of the books, papers, articles, technical reports, etc., consulted by one or more of the authors during the preparation of this study; bibliographic entries appearing elsewhere in this book are not repeated here.

ACM. 1974. A problem-list of issues concerning computers and public policy. Report of the ACM Committee on Computers and Public Policy. *Comm. ACM* **17**(9):495-503.

Allan, R. 1976. Components: Microprocessors galore. *IEEE Spectrum* **13**(1):50-56.

Amara, R. 1974. Toward understanding the social impact of computers. Report R-29. 2740 Sand Hill Rd., Menlo Park, CA 94025: Institute for the Future.

Amelio, G. F. 1975. Charge-coupled devices for memory applications. *Proc. AFIPS National Computer Conference,* vol. 44, pp. 515-22.

Armstrong, R. M. 1973. *Modular programming in COBOL.* New York: Wiley-Interscience.

Aronson, D. 1973. Key to tape/disk: Keys to user savings. *Electronic News* **18**(933):48-52 (July 23).

Auerbach. 1973a. European computer industry: Alive and well and expanding. *Auerbach Reporter* (February). Philadelphia: Auerbach Publishers.

————. 1973b. Data entry: More new answers to the same old problems. *Auerbach Reporter* (March). Philadelphia: Auerbach Publishers.

Baker, F. T. 1972. Chief programmer team management of production programming. *IBM Systems Journal* **11**(1):56-73.

Balzer, R. M. 1972. Automatic programming. Institute Technical Memorandum. Marina del Rey, CA 90291: Information Sciences Institute, Univ. of Southern Calif.

————, Greenfield, N. R., Kay, M. J., Mann, W. C., and Ryder, W. R. 1974. Domain-independent automatic programming. Report ISI-RR-73-14. Marina del Rey, CA 90291: Information Sciences Institute, Univ. of Southern Calif.

Barnes, G. H., Brown, R. M., Kato, M., Kuck, D. J., Slotnick, D. L., and Stokes, R. A. 1968. The ILLIAC IV computer. *IEEE Trans. on Computers* **17**(8):746-57.

Bemer, R. W., ed. 1971. *Computers and crises: How computers are shaping our future.* New York: Association for Computing Machinery.

Benjamin, R. I. 1971. *Control of the information system development cycle.* New York: Wiley-Interscience.

Bjerrum, C. A. 1969. Forecast of computer developments and applications 1968-2000. *Futures* **1**(4):331-38.

Boulding, K. 1968. *Beyond economics.* Ann Arbor, MI: Univ. of Michigan Press.

Bowers, D. M. 1973. Predicting future computer developments. *Modern Data* **6**(5):62-68.

Brandon, D. H., and Gray, M. 1970. *Project control standards.* Philadelphia: Brandon Systems.

Bromberg, H. 1970. Software buying. *Datamation* 16(11):35-40.

Burroughs Corp. 1973. *Problem oriented language generator (POLGEN) reference manual.* Burroughs Place, Detroit, MI 48232: Burroughs Corp.

Byrne, B., Mullally, A., and Rothery, B. 1971. *The art of systems analysis.* Englewood Cliffs, NJ: Prentice-Hall.

Canning, R. G. 1972a. COBOL aid packages. *EDP Analyzer* 10(5):1-14.

———. 1972b. Modular COBOL programming. *EDP Analyzer* 10(7):1-14.

———, and Sisson, R. L. 1967. *The management of data processing.* New York: Wiley.

Cashman, M. W. 1973. A read/write optical memory system. *Datamation* 19(3):66-69.

Christensen, G. S., and Jones, P. D. 1972. The Control Data Star-100 file storage station. *Proc. AFIPS Fall Joint Computer Conference,* vol. 41, pt. I, pp. 561-69.

Clifton, H. D. 1970. *Systems analysis for business data processing.* Philadelphia: Auerbach Publishers.

Cohen, A. 1972. Modular programs: Defining the module. *Datamation* 18(1):34-37.

Collins, B. D., and Acker, N. B. 1970. Documentation and debugging. *Data Management* 8(9):107-15.

Couger, J. D. 1973a. Evolution of business system analysis techniques. *Computing Surveys* 5(3):167-98.

———. 1973b. Curriculum recommendations for undergraduate programs in information systems. *Comm. ACM* 16(12):727-49.

———, ed. 1975. Annual bibliography of computer-oriented books, 8th ed. *Computing Newsletter for Instructors of Data Processing* 8(5):1-18. Colorado Springs, CO 80933: Center for Cybernetics Systems Synergism.

Cuozzo, D. E., and Kurtz, J. F. 1973. Building a base for data base: A management perspective. *Datamation* 19(10):71-75.

Curtis, D. A. 1971. Mass memory technologies. Part I: An overview; Part II: Magnetic systems; Part III: Electronic and beam deflection systems. *Instruments and Control Systems* 44(10):107-9; 44(11):82-87; 44(12):80-82.

Dahl, O. J., Dijkstra, E. W., and Hoare, C. A. R. 1972. *Structured programming.* New York: Academic Press.

Davidow, W. H. 1972. The rationale for logic from semiconductor memory. *Proc. AFIPS Spring Joint Computer Conference,* vol. 40, pp. 353-58.

De Greene, K. B., ed. 1970. *Systems psychology.* New York: McGraw-Hill.

Doll, D. R. 1974. Telecommunications turbulence and the computer network evolution. *Computer* 7(2):13-22.

EDP Industry Report. 1972. 360/370 migration. *EDP Industry Report* 8(3):1-4.

Electronic News. 1972. Computer trends fall 1972. *Electronic News* 27(900): section 2:1-40 (December 4).

Engelbart, D. C., Watson, R. W., and Norton, J. C. 1973. The augmented knowledge workshop. *Proc. AFIPS National Computer Conference,* vol. 42, pp. 9-21.

Falk, H. 1975. Computers. *IEEE Spectrum* 12(4):46-49.

———. 1976. Computers: Poised for progress. *IEEE Spectrum* 13(1):44-49.

Feidelman, L. 1971. *Data entry today.* 22929 Industrial Drive East, St Clair Shores, MI 48080: Management Information Services.

Frank, R. A. 1972. Special Report: Output techniques. *Computerworld* **6**(14):8-9 (April 5); **6**(15):8-9 (April 12); **6**(16):10-11 (April 19); **6**(17):8-9 (April 26).

Gallagher, J. D. 1973. Crystal balling: The corporate computer in the 70's. *Infosystems* **20**(1):24-25,58-59.

Gibson, C. F., and Nolan, R. L. 1974. Managing the four stages of EDP growth. *Harvard Business Review* **52**(1):76-88.

Gilchrist, B., and Weber, R. E. 1974. Enumerating full-time programmers. *Comm. ACM* **17**(10):592-93.

Gildersleeve, T. R. 1970. *Decision tables and their practical application in data processing.* Englewood Cliffs, NJ: Prentice-Hall.

———. 1971. *Design of sequential file systems.* New York: Wiley-Interscience.

Goetz, M. A. 1973. Soup-up your programmers with COBOL aids. *Computer Decisions* **5**(3):8-12.

Goldberg, J., ed. 1973. *Proc. Symposium on the High Cost of Software.* Menlo Park, CA 94025: Stanford Research Institute. Distributed by the National Technical Information Service (NTIS), U.S. Dept. of Commerce, Arlington, VA 22217 (AD 777 121).

Goodenough, J. B. 1972. Interim report: System organization technology. Waltham, MA 02154: Softech, Inc.

———, and Eanes, R. S. 1972. Interim report: Program testing and diagnosis technology. Waltham, MA 02154: Softech, Inc.

———, and Ross, D. T. 1972. An analysis of modularity. Waltham, MA 02154: Softech, Inc.

Gray, M., and London, K. R. 1969. *Documentation standards.* Philadelphia: Brandon Systems.

Greenberg, S. 1972. *GPSS primer.* New York: Wiley-Interscience.

Grenier, E. J., Jr., Martin, F. J., Jr., and Winkler, R. L. 1974. Liability for breaches of computer data security: How courts consider standards of care and technological feasibility. *Proc. Second International Conference on Computer Communications,* pp. 457-67. Stockholm: International Council of ICCC. (Order from International Council on Computer Communications, P. O. Box 9745, Washington, DC 20016).

GUIDE. 1972. The data base administrator. Data Base Administration Project Report. 111 E. Wacker Dr., Chicago, IL 60601: GUIDE International.

———. 1973. Requirements for a user language. Data Base User Language Project Report. 111 E. Wacker Dr., Chicago, IL 60601: GUIDE International.

Hamilton, W. R. 1971. Tracking project progress. *Data Processing Magazine* **13**(9):36-37.

Head, R. V. 1971. *Guide to packaged systems.* New York: Wiley.

Hetzel, W. C., ed. 1973. *Program test methods.* Englewood Cliffs, NJ: Prentice-Hall.

Hoagland, A. S. 1973. Mass storage: Past, present, and future. *Computer* **6**(9):29-33.

Hodges, D. A. 1973. Alternative component technologies for advanced memory systems. *Computer* **6**(9):35-37.

Horowitz, J. 1970. Effective planning with CPM. *Journal of Systems Management* **21**(3):27-29.

Houston, G. B. 1973. Trillion bit memories. *Datamation* **19**(10):52-58.

IBM. 1971. The chief programmer team: Principles and procedures. Report Number FSC 71-5108. Gaithersburg, MD 20760: Federal Systems Division, IBM Corp.

————. 1972. The considerations of physical security in a computer environment. Form No. G520-2700. 1133 Westchester Ave., White Plains, NY 10604: IBM Corp.

————. 1973. Organizing the data processing installation. Form GC20-1622-2. 1133 Westchester Ave., White Plains, NY 10604: IBM Corp.

IEEE Spectrum. 1974. Computer report. *IEEE Spectrum* **11**(2):Special issue.

Infodata Systems, Inc. 1968. INQUIRE: Installation and operation guide, user's guide. 5205 Leesburg Pike, Falls Church, VA 22041: Infodata Systems.

Informatics, Inc. 1974. MARK IV: User and operation guides. Change 3.0. P. O. Box 1452, Canoga Park, CA 91304: Mark IV Systems Co.

Jacobs, R. A. 1972. Putting "manage" into project management. *Journal of Systems Management* **23**(1):20-25.

Jardine, D. A., ed. 1974. *Data base management systems (Proc. 1973 SHARE Working Conference on Data Base Management Systems).* New York: American Elsevier.

John Hoskyns and Company, Ltd. 1973. *Implications of using modular programming.* Central Computer Agency Guide No. 1. London: Her Majesty's Stationary Office. (Available in the U.S. from Hoskyns Research Inc., 600 Third Ave., New York, NY 10016).

Johnson, L. R. 1970. *System structure in data, programs, and computers.* Englewood Cliffs, NJ: Prentice-Hall.

Jones, P. A. 1971. The computer: A cost-benefit analysis. *Management Accounting* **53**(1):23-25,51.

Joslin, E. O. 1968. *Computer selection.* Reading, MA: Addison-Wesley.

————. 1971. Costing the systems design alternatives. *Data Management* **9**(4):23-27.

Kernighan, B. W., and Plauger, P. J. 1974. *The elements of programming style.* New York: McGraw-Hill.

Knuth, D. 1969-73. *The art of computer programming;* vol. I: *Fundamental algorithms,* 2nd ed. 1973; vol. II: *Seminumerical algorithms,* 1969; vol. III: *Sorting and searching,* 1973. Reading, MA: Addison-Wesley.

————. 1974. Computer programming as an art. *Comm. ACM* **17**(12):667-73.

Krauss, L. I. 1969. *Administering and controlling the company data processing function.* Englewood Cliffs, NJ: Prentice-Hall.

Laliotis, T. A. 1973. Main memory technology. *Computer* **6**(9):19-27.

Lucas, H. C., Jr. 1971. A user-oriented approach to systems design. *Proc. ACM 1971 Annual Conference,* pp. 325-38. New York: Association for Computing Machinery.

Lyon, J. K. 1971. *An introduction to data base design.* New York: Wiley-Interscience.

McCracken, D. D. 1972. *A guide to FORTRAN IV programming,* 2nd ed. New York: Wiley-Interscience.

————, and Garbassi, U. 1970. *A guide to COBOL programming,* 2nd ed. New York: Wiley-Interscience.

McFarlan, F. W., Nolan, R. L., and Norton, D. P. 1973. *Information systems administration.* New York: Holt.

McKay, K. G. 1971. Digital communications: A tutorial. *Bell Laboratories Record* **49**(9):278-84.

McLaughlin, R. A. 1974. A survey of 1974 dp budgets. *Datamation* **20**(2)52-56.

Martin, J. 1965. *Programming real-time computer systems.* Englewood Cliffs, NJ: Prentice-Hall.

————. 1970. *Teleprocessing network organization.* Englewood Cliffs, NJ: Prentice-Hall.

————. 1973. *Design of man-computer dialogues.* Englewood Cliffs, NJ: Prentice-Hall.

Martino, J. P. 1972. *Technological forecasting for decision-making.* New York: American Elsevier.

————, ed. 1972. *Introduction to technological forecasting.* New York: Gordon & Breach.

Mitroff, I. I. 1971. A communication model of dialectical inquiring systems: A strategy for strategic planning. *Management Science: Application Series* **17**(10):B634-48.

Moder, J. J., and Phillips, C. R. 1970. *Project management with CPM and PERT,* 2nd ed. New York: Van Nostrand.

Molnar, J. P. 1971. The telephone plant of the 1970's. *Bell Laboratories Record* **49**(1):2-12.

Naftaly, S. M., Cohen, M. C., and Johnson, B. G. 1972. *COBOL support packages: Programming and productivity aids.* New York: Wiley-Interscience.

Packer, D. W. 1970. Effective program design. *Computers & Automation* **19**(7):37-41.

Pollack, S. L., Hicks, H. T., Jr., and Harrison, W. J. 1971. *Decision tables: Theory and practice.* New York: Wiley-Interscience.

Reichenbach, R. R., and Tasso, C. A. 1968. *Organizing for data processing.* AMA Research Study 92. New York: American Management Association.

Rubin, M. L. 1970a. *Handbook of data processing management,* vol. I: *Introduction to the system life cycle.* Philadelphia: Brandon Systems.

————. 1970b. *Handbook of data processing management,* vol. II: *System life cycle standards.* Philadelphia: Brandon Systems.

————, ed. 1970c. *Handbook of data processing management,* vol. IV: *Advanced technology—Input and output.* Philadelphia: Auerbach Publishers.

Rudolph, J. A. 1972. A production implementation of an associative array processor: STARAN. *Proc. AFIPS Fall Joint Computer Conference,* vol. 41, pt. I, pp. 229-41.

Rustin, R., ed. 1971. *Debugging techniques in large systems: Courant Computer Science Symposium 1.* Englewood Cliffs, NJ: Prentice-Hall.

Sackman, H. 1967. *Computers, systems science, and evolving society: The challange of man-machine digital systems.* New York: Wiley.

Salzman, R. M. 1971. An outlook for the terminal industry in the United States. *Computer* **4**(6):18-25.

Schroeder, W. J. 1972. How to shop for software. *Business Automation* **19**(5):20-23.

Seligman, L. 1972. LSI and minicomputer system architecture. *Proc. AFIPS Spring Joint Computer Conference,* vol. 40, pp. 767-73.

Sharpe, W. F. 1969. *The economics of computers.* New York: Columbia Univ. Press.

Turnblade, R. C. 1971. The case for dedicated computers. *Data Processing Magazine* **13**(5):41-44.

U.S. Air Force. 1971. *Information processing/data automation implications of Air Force command and control requirements in the 1980's (CCIP-85).* Los Angeles, CA: U.S. Air Force Space and Missile Systems Organization.

U.S. Bureau of Census. 1973. *Census of population 1970, detailed characteristics, final report PC(1)-D1, United States summary.* Washington, DC 20402: U.S. Government Printing Office.

―――. 1974. *Characteristics of persons in engineering and scientific occupations: 1972.* Technical paper No. 33. Washington, DC 20402: U.S. Government Printing Office.

U.S. Department of Commerce. 1975. *U.S. industrial outlook with projections to 1985.* Washington, DC 20402: U.S. Government Printing Office.

U.S. Department of Labor. 1970. *Patterns of U.S. economic growth.* Bureau of Labor Statistics Bulletin 1672. Washington, DC 20402: U.S. Government Printing Office.

―――. 1974. *The U.S. economy in 1985: A summary of BLS projections.* Bureau of Labor Statistics Bulletin 1809. Washington, DC 20402: U.S. Government Printing Office.

von Bertalanffy, L. 1968. *General system theory: Foundations, development, applications.* New York: George Braziller.

Wallace, J. B., Jr. 1972. Improving communications between systems analyst and user. *Data Management* 10(6):21-24.

Weber, E., Teal, G. K., and Schillinger, A. G., eds. 1971. *Technology forecast for 1980.* New York: Van Nostrand Reinhold.

Weinberg, G. M. 1966. *PL/I programming primer.* New York: McGraw-Hill.

―――. 1971. *The psychology of computer programming.* New York: Van Nostrand Reinhold.

White House Conference Staff. 1972. *A look at business in 1990: A summary of the conference.* Proc. White House Conference on the Industrial World Ahead. Washington, DC 20402: U.S. Government Printing Office.

Wilkinson, S. 1973. *The stainless steel carrot.* Boston: Houghton Mifflin.

Withington, F. G. 1972. The next (and last?) generation. *Datamation* 18(5):71-74.

―――. 1973.. Crystal balling: Trends in EDP management. *Infosystems* 20(1):20-21.

―――. 1974. Five generations of computers. *Harvard Business Review* 52(4):99-108.

Zuckerman, P. 1970. *Handbook of data processing management,* vol. III: *System life cycle standards—Forms method.* Philadelphia: Brandon Systems.

INDEX

Academic curricula, and data processing professionals. *See* Education
Accounting, for computer usage, 122-24
Adaptability, of data processing systems, 156
Administrative support services, 134-36
  and data processing services, *compared,* Table 7.1
Applications, 53-64
  automatic generation of, 113-15
  batch, 54
  business and commercial, 53-54, 57-61
  design of, by mid user, 46
  end users' requirements for, 46
  in education, 53, 60
  government, 53, 58, 60
  implementation of, by mid user, 47
  installation of, by mid user, 47-48
  interactive, 55, 57
  maintenance of, by mid user, 48
  military, 53
  for office automation, 57, 134-36
  for planning, 56-57
  process-control, 61
  produced by end users, 112-13
  real-time, 5, 53
  scientific, 55
  sensor-driven, 58
  for supporting top management, 56-57
  testing of, by mid user, 47
Applications development, 45-48
  and computer installations, 130-34
  productivity of, 105-8, 157-59
Applications programmers, 7, 92. *See also* Mid users
Apprenticeship, in the programming craft, 25, 131
Assumptions, of forecast, 12-13
Automation
  of office work, 57, 134-36
  and "work ethic," 21-22
Availability, of data processing systems, 5, 45, 69-72, 155-56

Businesses. *See* Enterprises

Cable area television (CATV), 63, 77
CATV. *See* Cable area television
Central processor (CPU). *See* Hardware, central processor
Clayton Act, 15
Communications facilities, 76-78
  in business applications, 58-59
  and computer networks, 81
  for home computers, 64
Computer networks, 81-82
  and business operations, 132
  and software implementation, 112
Computer programs. *See* Software
Computers
  in the home, 61-64, 80
  number of, Table B.2
Costs, of data processing. *See* Data processing, economics of
CPU. *See* Hardware, central processor
Craft. *See* Programming, as a craft
Customers. *See* Users

Data
  capture of, by business applications, 57, 59
  custody of, in corporations, 121-22
  projected quantities of, 28-29
Data banks, 15
Data-base systems, 19, 111-12
  and business applications, 129
  and computer networks, 112
  distributed, 117, 158
  growth of, 29, 74
  and home computers, 64
  interfaces between applications and, 157
  requirement for, 59
  storage for, 74
  and system support users, 133
Data processing
  and administrative support services, *compared,* Table 7.1